Cragg, Kenneth
   Alive to God; Muslim and Christian prayer,
compiled with an introductory essay by Kenneth
Cragg.   London, Oxford University Press, 1970.
   xiv, 194 p.   20 cm.

   "Sources": p. 173-183.

1. Prayers.   2. Islam. Prayers.   I. Title.

ALIVE TO GOD

MUSLIM AND CHRISTIAN PRAYER

ALIVE TO GOD

MUSLIM AND CHRISTIAN PRAYER

compiled
with an Introductory Essay by
KENNETH CRAGG

LONDON

OXFORD UNIVERSITY PRESS
NEW YORK   TORONTO
1970

Oxford University Press, Ely House, London W.1

GLASGOW NEW YORK TORONTO MELBOURNE WELLINGTON
CAPE TOWN SALISBURY IBADAN NAIROBI DAR ES SALAAM LUSAKA ADDIS ABABA
BOMBAY CALCUTTA MADRAS KARACHI LAHORE DACCA
KUALA LUMPUR SINGAPORE HONG KONG TOKYO

SBN 19 213220 2

Printed in Great Britain by
Billing & Sons Limited, Guildford and London

for
MELITA

Preface

This book is a search for community which derives, nevertheless, from a sense that it is already there. 'I have been way down yonder in the valley by myself,' wrote James Baldwin, 'where I couldn't hear nobody pray, except occasionally me.' Any sensitive person knows what he means. Yet there is nothing private about the instinct to pray, to move with the world's perplexities towards a belief in responsibility there beyond us, and yet also recruiting us. The instinct is inseparable from our experience of the human situation, whose tragedies matter only because its glory is real. In its deepest quality the will to pray is simply being human seriously and inclusively. It is being alive imaginatively.

Yet the great formal systems of religion are by tradition so massively separatist, so exclusive in their patterns and concepts, participant, as it were, only in and with themselves and with the cultures they inhabit, that any mutuality between them requires constant initiative and arouses strong misgiving.

This work is a modest venture in such mutuality between two adjacent, yet historically hostile, faiths. It had its beginnings in Jerusalem in the late fifties and has been in process all through the sixties in Cairo and Canterbury, Ibadan and New York, and finally in Cambridge, and is the fruit of many roots of thought and reading and friendship. The prayers gave rise to the reflections which the Introduction sets down: the convictions in the Introduction sustained and justified the sense of valid, if partial, kinship created by the prayers. These, it is fair to say, collected themselves. I was all the time discovering Christian writers unconsciously sharing Islamic phrases and vocabulary, and Muslim writers, for their part echoing, for example, the *Magnificat* and moving, unawares, within a Christian orbit. It was a relatively simple matter to gather these. They evidently deserved a common roof for their habitation.

It is obvious that these implicit unities of heart have their hinterlands of theology where there is explicit contradiction and discordancy. These, with the problems of authority and of finality that inhabit them, are frankly faced and pondered in the Introduction. But we shall most truly care for what involves a loyal controversy, if we genuinely possess in common what is properly so. If only fears rule our attitudes, how shall they be the attitudes of faiths? There can be no real loyalty where there is only isolation.

But the anthology ranges outside theism and affirmation, into the wistfulness of sceptics and the bleak honesties of negation. For these are an authentic school of prayer, asking as they do the questions that must penetrate every sanctuary. There are many in our time for whom prayer cannot be more than a direction of thought and will towards compassion, and that, universally. Too many words, too great an assurance of phrase, are then uncongenial. We can perhaps only set ourselves to will, in the world, the work of love. Perhaps we say with John Keats, in his last, still youthful, struggle with disease: 'I will be as believing in love as I am able.' And the ability does not fully carry us into the language of established worship. This, it may be, is more alive to God just by being less confidently so. We, therefore, make room attentively for those who pray by the very force of their distrust of prayer. We need them no less than the great practitioners of the presence of God.

Each page in the sections of Praise, Penitence, and Petition, is meant to be a unity. Succeeding themes are mainly on adjacent pages. The Index is not meant to be exhaustive. Prayers not otherwise noted for source are by the present author, as are the translations of the Qur'ān. The dedication breathes the grateful gladness of the poem to which the reader may turn on p. 145. 'Words', anyway, as William Burroughs wrote in another connection, 'are an ox-cart way of doing things . . . clumsy instruments.' But even an ox-cart can be capacious, with strength and perseverance in its harness, and always close to the soil and the toil, and the hope and the harvest.

Gonville and Caius College   KENNETH CRAGG
Cambridge
January, 1970

Acknowledgements

Acknowledgement is made to the following publishers and copyright owners for permission to use extracts from the under-mentioned works. Fuller details of authors and sources are on pages 159–183.

A. J. Arberry, *Tales from the Masnavi*: George Allen and Unwin Ltd.

Abubakar Tafawa Balewa, *Shaihi Umar*: Longmans Green and Co. Ltd. (U.S.A.: Humanities Press Inc.).

The Travels of Ibn Jubayr, translated by R. J. C. Broadhurst: Jonathan Cape Ltd.

Albert Camus, *The Fall*: copyright 1956 Editions Gallimard, Hamish Hamilton; translation copyright 1957, Justin O'Brien.

Caribbean Voices, Vol. I, edited by John Figueroa: Evans Bros.

The Book of Common Prayer: Crown copyright, reprinted by permission.

Basil Dowling, *Signs and Wonders* (Caxton Press, New Zealand), by permission of the author.

Early Christian Prayers, edited by Adalbert Hamman, translated from the German by W. Mitchell: Longmans Green and Co. Ltd.

Frantz Fanon, *Black Skin, White Masks*, translated from the French by C. L. Markham: MacGibbon and Kee Ltd. (U.S.A.: Grove Press Inc.).

Shams al-Dīn Ḥāfiẓ, *Fifty Poems of Ḥafiz*, translated by A. J. Arberry: Cambridge University Press.

Dag Hammarskjöld, *Markings*, translated by Leif Sjöberg and W. H. Auden: Faber and Faber Ltd. (U.S.A.: Alfred A. Knopf Inc.).

John Hoyland, *The Fourfold Sacrament*: W. Heffer and Sons Ltd.

Kamil Hussain, *City of Wrong*, translated by Kenneth Cragg: Djambatan Publishers, Holland.

Muḥammad Iqbāl, *Jāvid Nāmā*, translated by A. J. Arberry: George Allen and Unwin Ltd.

Ibn Ḥazm, *The Ring of the Dove*, translated by A. J. Arberry: Luzac and Co. Ltd.

Søren Kierkegaard, *Journals* (translated by Alexander Dru), by permission of the translator.

ix

Contents

Introductory Essay

> There is scarce truth enough alive, to make societies secure,
> but security enough to make fellowships accurs'd. Much upon
> this riddle runs the wisdom of this world. This news is old
> enough, yet it is every day's news.[1]

Old enough, too, as the habit of the centuries. Cultures and
religions relate themselves defensively to the rest of mankind,
believing in their identity as the service of the truth—a conviction
which, at the same time, reserves them from the human whole to
which their truth belongs. Common tragedies of evil afflict their
interior societies and beckon them into the wider wholeness of the
world. But the impulse to the inward conservation of themselves
suspects and refuses the pressures of a larger fellowship and, all
too confidently—yet not confidently enough—they 'salute their
brethren only'.

Such deliberate avoidance in the spirit has long, and generally,
been characteristic of Islam and Christianity. The time is ready
for an equally deliberate will towards a mutual engagement in the
world. The common prayers of Muslims and Christians in these
pages are brought together in this cause. Moving from these
proved affinities of soul, the aim of this Introductory Essay is to
suggest and justify the possibility of their more active expression
among Christians and Muslims responsively to their separate
convictions and to the urgencies of the contemporary scene.

Islam and Christianity, it is fair to say, are deep and inclusive
patterns of the cognizance of God. They can properly be seen as
adjacent faiths. For all their taxing diversities and tensions they
have in common a vital sense of the Lordship of the worlds. The

---

[1] William Shakespeare: *Measure for Measure*, Act 3, Sc. 1, line 214 f.

phrase 'alive to God' is certainly descriptive of their kindred and contrasted patterns of devotion, however carefully we shall need, below, to ponder that 'quarrel in God's nature',[1] which divides them. That there is a third, and prior, partner in their mono-theism is in no way forgotten, nor are the claims of every other faith-system. The integrity of every religion is at stake in its awareness of them all. A dual venture may, nevertheless, be seen as a token of a wider task and perhaps its only readily manageable form. Other reasons for our present concentration on a twofold intercourse of soul will find their place in a later paragraph.

This modest volume had its genesis, over more than a decade, in the evident kinships existing between Muslim and Christian devotion as these impressed themselves unsought upon a single observer, at first casually and carelessly, and then, at length, inviting, under the weight of discovery, an active compilation. The book is, therefore, not so much an essay with appended evidence, as evidence with a prefaced explanation. Its two parts, to be sure, inter-depend. But there is no case to make for it unless it makes its own. Fragmentary and preliminary as it is, it bears witness to what is irrefutably present in the prayers of the two faiths and to something that, in wiser hands and keener spirits, is capable of ample enlargement. In a measure, Muslims and Christians, or some of them, have been praying together for centuries. For they have been moving, divergently but still relevantly, in many kindred themes.

It is, however, the antipathies which dominate the story of their relationships. In liturgy and sacrament they have belonged in sharply sundered camps. It is their own they summon to their own. 'Let *us* pray' runs the familiar Christian invitation. 'Thee it is *we* worship' says the opening Surah of the Qur'ān. The inten-tion, in either case, is the proper community, whether of the church or of the mosque, to the firm, even scornful, exclusion of the improper one. Whatever mundane exchanges have been feasible or necessary between the parties, supra-mundane fellow-ships have rarely found a place. It has been as with old Shylock in the play: 'I will buy with you, sell with you, walk with you,

---

[1] A phrase of Christopher Fry in *The Firstborn*.

talk with you . . . but I will not pray with you.'[1] His sentiments are everywhere echoed among the faithful in the faiths. The verb 'to pray', it seems, does not take the preposition 'with' except on the strictest conditions of identity,[2] conditions often fortified by massive prejudice or sheltering an introspective and self-regarding piety.

> 'Twas the hour when rites unholy
> Called each Paynim voice to prayer[3]

wrote an English poet, loftily, of the muezzin. For the godly Ibn Jubayr, returning from the Meccan pilgrimage late in A.D. 1184, the Frankish Christian occupation of Acre, with its mosques, was 'ravishment' and 'defilement'. He wrote with mingled wistfulness and unconcealed dismay of one mosque in the east of the town, where the *miḥrāb*, or niche marking the direction of Mecca, remained so that

Muslim and infidel assemble there, the one turning to his place of worship, the other to his . . .

where 'pigs [Christians] and crosses abound'.[4] And, some weary weeks later, after surviving with the most of some two thousand Christian pilgrims in the perils of a Mediterranean voyage in a Rumi (Greek) ship, he found his deliverance and its common human gratefulness marred by the sight of Messina

. . . the mart of merchant infidels. . . . Teeming with worshippers of the Cross, it chokes its inhabitants and constricts them almost to strangling. It is full of smells and filth and churlish too, for the stranger there will find no courtesy.

Yet he was lively enough also to note that the *ʿalamah*, or ensign motto of William, King of Sicily, was the Islamic inscription: 'Praise be to God. It is proper to praise Him', while the king's

---

[1] William Shakespeare: *The Merchant of Venice*, Act 1, Sc. 3, line 32 f.
[2] In respect, that is, of fellowship. One may well pray *with* fervour inside the 'right' community.
[3] Thomas Campbell: *The Turkish Lady*.
[4] *The Travels of Ibn Jubayr*, trans. by R. J. C. Broadhurst, London, 1952, pp. 318–19.

father's had been: 'Praise be to God in thanks for his beneficence.'[1]

It was doubtless beyond the power or the circumstance of those centuries to have it otherwise, save in the rarest of exceptions. Even where, as for example with Luther, there was a meed of recognition it made no difference to the fundamental hostility.

The Turks . . . pray with such decency, quietness and fine outward decorum, as can be found nowhere in our churches. . . . You will observe a strict, courageous and respectable conduct among the Turks, so far as their outward life is concerned.[2]

None the less 'the conscience must be fortified against the rites of Muḥammad' and the wiles of *Alcoran.*

Can all this stubborn history be feasibly reversed? Is there any ground for the notion, much less for the hope, that these powerful and competing identities of mosque and church can ever find a real togetherness? Are not the doctrines within them and the centuries behind them in fact prevailing and pervading realities which may perhaps learn to be conciliatory but can never expect to be conciliated? Is there not about each of them a necessary militancy towards the other, without which neither could be itself, since what is between them is inherently a study in contrasts? Cathedrals may have been turned into mosques, from the great Saint Sophia to remote Dunqala in the Sudan,[3] and, more rarely, mosques into cathedrals, from Acre to Algiers. But the soul of things has never tarried through these dispossessions. Are we not faced with an otherness which cannot be reduced, abated, merged, or interchanged?

There is no denying the force and cogency of these questions and no disputing the toughness of the facts within them. But the present case does not proceed by doing so. On the contrary, the point of crucial concern is best made by insisting that no abeyance of what church and mosque, Gospel and Qur'ān, mean to their

---

[1] *The Travels of Ibn Jubayr,* pp. 338, 341.

[2] See E. M. Plass: *What Luther Says: an Anthology,* 1959, Vol. 2, 3025 f.

[3] See the recent study of the passing away of Christianity in the medieval Sudan in Yusuf Faḍl Ḥasan: *The Arabs and the Sudan,* Edinburgh, 1967.

proper communities is here in view. Rather the mutuality for which we argue presupposes their continuity as a necessity of its own hopes. Something has to happen to the temper of that continuity, to be sure, but the fact of it must remain the basis of all else. The prayers which, it is believed, this collection shows to possess a dual citizenship could only have arisen, and can only still arise, from within an unbroken life of devotion belonging to their separate origins.

Many perplexities will be circumvented if this situation is kept constantly in mind. No fusion of corporate acts of worship and *'ibādāt* is intended. There is no question of taking Sunday for Friday, or Friday for Sunday.[1] Ramaḍān and Holy Week, Quranic chant and Eucharist, the sacrament of prostration and the sacrament of oblation, remain the foci of great alternative responses to the Divine majesty depending on deep, alternative alertness to the Divine Name, as the respective theologies believe they have received their revelation of it. Without these distinctive and familiar worlds of liturgy and cultic life, there will be no independent vitality to bring into mutual relation and, in that sense, even the common territory will disappear. For it is not even common unless it is authentically possessed. And there is no such Muslim or Christian possession which does not dwell also with controversy and contrast.

'The readiness', we may say, 'is all'—readiness born of separate loyalties and alive to God in the summons we hear from the world about us, from contemporary history and the technological opportunity, from plural mankind and shared nationhood, from a score of strenuous situations in the common fields of social justice, welfare, education and the rest. All such demands and occasions, in their impact, bring our prostration or our oblation, our Qurʾān recital and our Holy Communion, before the same bar of mercy and compassion toward a harassed and a wistful world, before the same criteria of our neighbour for the Lord's sake. They prompt us, within and yet outside our continuing canonical and traditional acts of worship, to ventures of common

---

[1] Except in the strict calendar sense when legal holidays determine the days and hours of employment and so the feasible occasions of religious observance and festival.

consecration and a joint seeking of 'the face of God', whether in
vital silence, or in shared vocabulary. Our inward loyalties must
mean exterior relationships. We are not alive to God if we are
dead to each other. In our sort of world the care of prayer has
become a calling we cannot answer only in isolation.

2

For there is no longer any isolated world. Endlessly plural
diversities there are, truly. But they now possess a unity of
circumstance, a convergence of history, such as no previous
generations knew. Mosques, synagogues, temples, churches, all
persist in their manifold variety. The races, peoples, territories,
societies and cultures of man keep and sharpen their ancient and
separate identities. But around these insistent pluralisms flow the
same tides of science, the same currents of technology and change.
Oceans, deserts, and mountain ranges are denied their former
power to sunder the communities of men. They are so readily
crossed or so effectively ignored. Seclusions arising from geography are passing altogether into history. Economic disparities,
tragically, grow more chronic. The poor are contrasted with the
rich, the hungry with the affluent, more cruelly and certainly
more widely than in any earlier time. But even wealth and poverty
breed this grim *apartheid* within an actual oneness that now makes
responsibility worldwide. The sort of contrasts which burned
themselves into the conscience of Karl Marx in the nineteenth
century, as he brooded over the tragedy of industrial England,
have now become global in their incidence, and their correction,
if it is to be achieved, requires a terrestrial, not a merely national,
concert of policy and will. Whatever the answers, Communist or
otherwise, there are now no frontiers to delimit or simplify their
burden.

Such, unmistakably, is the current commonness of human
destiny and every angle of assessment confirms the case. There
is an urgent unity in our very discords. The nuclear cloud casts a

single shadow. Nations are no longer private to themselves. Space missions photograph our very unity and leave to imagination a planetary mission on the ground. What accentuates the paradox of all our enmities is the realization that they are ours as one—one globe, one history, one humanity.

Every culture in our time is thus becoming, in some sense, inter-cultural. Remote neighbourhoods and relatively static communities still, of course, persist, only partially open to the impact of travel and the impress of education. But even these are steadily penetrated by the ubiquitous agencies of modernity and subject to the inexorable pressures of a common science. Every continent makes its own uneasy negotiation with the new. For men cannot be unborn when they are old. But, in the flux of time, none can elude the dangers which technology authorizes, which the machine effectuates and which the city celebrates in pride and hides in squalor.

So it is that the present mould even of the distinctiveness of human families is one mould. In a recent biography, a Kikuyu sees himself as a 'child of two worlds' in one Kenya, while a Nigerian writer reminisces about his double nurture and employs the same phrase.[1] Uneasily, in one personality, the double past struggles with a new present. Examples are legion. Nor is race, for all its tenacity and passion, a force for exemption from the impact, as distinct from the prizes, of technology. The tragic folly of *apartheid* in South Africa, as Ezekiel Mphahlele has shown,[2] does not immunize the whites from the presence and authority of the Bantu races. Their very security makes their own fellowships accursed. It is both a folly and a crime to see race as ever making for a decisive or a final demarcator of mankind. Whatever policies may impose, the single identity of man persists, and where it is not welcomed in honest recognition, it stays to accuse and haunt the conspiracy of pride or power against it. We cannot well have our own humanity unless we confess it everywhere. In the end the

---

[1] R. Mugo Gatheru: *Child of Two Worlds*, London, 1964; and Dilim Okafor Omali: *A Nigerian Childhood in Two Worlds*, London, 1965. Cf. Hamidou Kane: *L'Aventure Ambigüe*, Paris, 1960.

[2] In *The African Image*, London, 1962, and in his autobiographical *Down Second Avenue*, London, 1959.

denial of a common humanity is the damnation of our own.
Nature leaves no ultimate privacies and now history is strenuously
confirming the same lesson.

In such a world and in such a time is it the role of religion only
to divide and insulate, to buttress pride and conspire with fear?
Can prayer only happen in segregated segments of mankind?
Must we always part before we can adore? Must the faiths ignore
this growing unification of our history—the history they claim to
comfort and interpret? Are the sanctuaries of the transcendent to
be only havens of the cowardly and the crabbed of soul?

> 'Do not you hear us speak?'
> 'I do, and surely it is a sleepy language.'[1]

Is this to be the kind of exchange between the men of religion and
the vigorous movers in our day and place? More particularly, are
Islam and Christianity to be only preoccupied with a traditional
counter-vigilance between themselves and, in their often mutual
societies and nations, negligent of the courage and the nervousness
of modern men and of the accelerating problems of their souls
and of their works?

There belongs here for all theism a task of deeply testing
quality. It can hardly be denied that prayer is its real crisis. Is it
not, in the end, the *lex orandi* rather than the *lex credendi* on which
the answer turns? Doctrine about God is, no doubt, crucial. But,
however careful and authentic, it is neutralized unless He is
acknowledged. It is more urgent to be alive to God than orthodox
about Him, in the sense that even ignorance may be retrieved, but
only when He is not ignored.

3

Here, of course, we encounter the contemporary assumptions
of human self-sufficiency, to which both Islam and Christianity
have such exacting duties. Our very empire in technology tends

[1] William Shakespeare: *The Tempest*, Act 2, Sc. 1, lines 200–1.

to the conviction that faith in God is an archaic irrelevance and finds a liberation in the exodus of the mistaken hypothesis of transcendence. Muslims and Christians are fundamentally committed to the belief that such accounts of man beyond God are false to the human glory itself and dangerously awry in their eager deconsecration of the world. For Biblical and Quranic faith, it is a tragic misreading of the truth of man to think that he is left to himself in the universe, required to live by his own devices in a gap that God used to fill. Such religionlessness quite misses the very significance of the science it alleges as its ground and misinterprets a magnificent mastery over things as a cosmic exclusion of all other lordship.

Science, indeed, only lives by deeply religious dimensions of integrity, submission, authority, and obligation. Its inventions and achievements reach out into realms of responsibility and referability to neighbours which are simply the other side of accountability to God. We have to learn to see the apparent 'absence' of God as the form, the liberating form, of his presence. The secular cannot be itself without the sacred. Worship can be seen as the only right and final context of the competence of man and the ultimate condition of what the Qur'ān calls the *amānah*, the human entrustment of the world into the hands of men.[1]

Yet the illusion of secularization which disavows this entrustment of being to man grows apace. It has an intoxicating quality and besets old societies with alarming speed, bewildering their static or obscurantist dogmas. In many segments of its human dispersion, Islam is critically involved in these stresses. They have been instinctively resisted in doctrinal circles, the temper of which has not readily taken the measure, or the complexity, of what is at stake, or has found refuge in merely negative repudiation. Muslim societies have strongly resistant powers of dogma, impervious, perhaps, but also imperturbable. 'The rapping of the west', wrote Akbar Ḥusain Allāhabādī, 'did not penetrate to the head. At least there was this strong point in favour of the turban.'[2] But, unwisely sustained, these solidities may only alienate the

---

[1] See Surah 33:72 where man 'bears' the trust of the universe.

[2] Quoted from Muhammad Sadiq: *History of Urdu Literature*, London, 1964, p. 313.

initiates of science, disserve the vocation of theology, fail the
vigorous precedents of Islamic thought and ensure a still more
explosive version of the crisis.

It takes time and nerve and wisdom for the ultimacies of true
religion to reassert themselves in the human spirit under the
all-submerging tide of material change. This is where we now are
in the human family, east and west, with a strenuous battle ahead
for the reality of God and the due dignity under God of human
kind. The struggle is one struggle: prayer is plainly its crux. We
cannot have the authentic status of man except we have also,
confessedly, the love and sovereignty of God. He is enthroned
upon the praises of his people: only in being surely his are they
truly their own.

To pray, then—to pray that we may pray—is the most vital
need of our generation, more so, not less so, because it is uniquely
aware of its power and singular in its crisis. Herein the West has
a peculiar onus. It has for so long been the source and stimulus of
secularity. We have honestly to wrestle with a consequent love/
hate relationship towards it, in a deep, psychological complication
of our common problem.[1] The nations with which Christianity
is historically associated have been the actual source of most of the
technological changes that have invaded the lands of Islam. The
latter have suffered inwardly by dint of the alien origin of these
disruptive and yet irreversible inroads, accompanied, notoriously,
as they are, by embittering political factors of empire, mandate,
and dominion and by vexing economic disequilibrium. In this
tangle, one possible corrective, attenuation, redemption—call it
what you will—with hope of a mutual recovery of common
fellowship as men would be the bridge of prayer. Whether east
or west, the servants of the Spirit need each other and 'Lord,
teach us to pray' is the essence of their need. 'When they question
you concerning Me', says the Qur'ān, 'say: "I am near to the

---

[1] The readiest example of this complex might be the poet, Muḥammad
Iqbāl (see below) who wrote: 'For all its repertory of varied charms, I will
take nothing from Europe except a warning.' *Jāvīd Nāmā*, trans. by
A. J. Arberry, London, 1966, lines 1169–70. The East was 'wasted by
the west's imperialism' (line 1031) yet had somehow to imitate its
dynamism.

caller when he calls. So let them pray" ' (Surah 2:186). The truest realism is to hold the questions of life open to the Divine answers and to do so through the whole range of both.

'So let them pray' is, then, no idle escapism. It is not an invitation to spirituality *against* technology. Nor is it the vested interests of institutional religion *against* the secular. On the contrary, it means the realization of a true humanity within the accomplishments and the perils of civilization. More utterly than ever before in history we have both blessing and destruction in our hands. They have need to be uplifted hands and, if uplifted, why not sometimes joined?

4

The case, however, does not turn only on these great *new* factors that make our situation urgent. It is not only an obligation for post-imperial relationships and the fascinating open questions of the space age. Faith is no less concerned with the age-old unity we have in simply being human. There is one, living, dying, quality about all mankind. Male and female, old and young, bound in the generations, set in families, hoping, fearing, yearning, striving, toiling, gaining, losing, having, getting, hating, loving—all these are one mortality through all times, faiths, and places. In this kinship men talk different languages: but they spell everywhere one humanity. This incorporation of all 'in Adam', this 'Adam' in all, we must fully confess. It is far more insistent than all the late-coming unifications of the scientists. Here, more than anywhere, we may find the springs of common prayer. For it is here we find the logic of a common frailty. Or, in the words of one of the most passionate of modern writers, a West Indian who gave his life to the Algerian resistance: -

I said that man is a Yes! I will never stop reiterating that. Yes! to life. Yes! to love! Yes! to generosity. But man is also a No! No! to scorn of man. No! to degradation of man. No! to exploitation of

man. . . . I recognize that I have one right alone—the right of
demanding human behaviour from the other. . . . I, a man of
colour, want only this. . . . That it be possible for me to discover
and love man, wherever he may be. Superiority, inferiority? why
not the quite simple attempt to touch the other, to feel the other,
to explain the other to myself?

I believe that the individual should be set to take on the universality inherent in the human condition.[1]

Or, again, in the nervous, rhetorical poetry of a fugitive soul, the
English William Cowper:

> . . . Pierce my vein,
> Take of the crimson stream meandering there,
> And catechize it well: apply thy glass,
> Search it, and prove it now if it be not blood
> Congenial with thine own: and, if it be,
> What edge of subtlety canst thou suppose . . .
> To cut the link of brotherhood, by which
> One common Maker bound me to the kind?[2]

It is out of such unity, and the inhumanities by which it is denied,
that we may learn the prayers of solidarity by which to seek the
God we have defied in all misusing of our fellows. Such care, at
once of penitence and participation, is implicit in the will to pray.
The Muslim and the Christian relationship is surely a fitting
place to sense and serve it. Any controversy, latent as it remains in
such a venture, will find the only proper context of its themes
when they are subdued to such practice of a single humanity as
the first meaning of the sovereign authority of God. Mankind
cannot be answerable to God only in dividedness, or answerable
for itself in closed circuits of devotion.

Yet is it not precisely prayers and forms of prayer that in fact
sunder and fragment humanity? 'Congregations', as we call them,
in mosque and church, are also 'segregations', credally and
liturgically bounded, following exclusive instincts and treasuring
differing patterns. These, as we have argued, will continue. But
can they not be opened in their sympathies and fulfilled, outside

[1] Frantz Fanon: *Black Skin, White Masks*, London, 1967, trans. from
the French of 1952, pp. 222, 231–2, 12.
[2] *The Task*, Book 3.

their inner shape, in some exterior relationships? Is it possible to find, within these separate continuities, a way, however brokenly, to bring together what they mean apart?

These large questions suggest a more practical and immediate enquiry. What actual circumstances are there to give precise incentive to the ultimate concerns? The answer, here at least, is readily to hand. Within the macrocosm of the world, there are many intimate situations in which Muslims and Christians find themselves. There are schools, colleges and universities, where a single context of work and study creates a shared community. There are hospitals with mixed staff and common duties to the sick and to research. May there not be in these a legitimate ground of common prayer? In wider spheres there are issues of single citizenship, of social action and of public conscience, which belong to all concerned, indifferently to their religious affiliation. Many nations of plural religious populations have a 'secular' basis in that citizenship is not identified with one faith, where majority and minority religions coexist and co-inhabit. Are there not, in such a situation, many needs and occasions calling for inter-religious action and, therefore, for inter-religious prayer to consecrate and sustain it?

Where official 'recognition' of the dominant faith obtains, there are almost everywhere important minorities whose integration is vital but where apathy and sullen timidity may enervate their forces. In contemporary politics the maturity and sanity of dominating religions and the liveliness and security of minority ones are alike urgent factors for the state, for society, and for the international community. These qualities may be fostered, or the hope of them confessed, by the will, however occasional, to bring an actual coexistence into spiritual expression.

In this inter-religious complex of state, education, society, commerce and government, there are the scholars and sociologists working on the problems of population, migration, development, industrialization, production, and the rest. Are these stakes of society in its responsible direction to be excluded from what is meant when worship is offered, or somehow first annexed to competing sanctuaries before they can be set under the Divine will?

Likewise, in their remoter fields, the theologians and the religious personnel. There has been, in some circles, a growing desire for dialogue between the faiths and between the sects within them, Orthodox, Catholic, Protestant, Anglican; Sunnī, Shīʿah, Ismāʿīlī, Aḥmadī. Such dialogue is broadly intellectual and doctrinal. It brings together the intention and interpretation of belief so that each may be understood in their own seriousness. Can this activity, with all its difficulty and precarious prospect, be rightly limited to discussion and to formulae? Is there not an equal, perhaps a prior, need for meeting, as far as may be, in the inner spirit of our faiths, as these are expressed and expressive in worship alone? If we are ready to talk about God shall we rightly avoid seeking him in unison? If there is properly a dialogue of faiths, can we exclude a community of reverence? Does the vocabulary of mutual explanation admit of no converse of soul?

Many will be unconvinced about these practical suggestions, daunted by their unfamiliarity or doubtful of their feasibility. There are those who instinctively shrink from what they fear may be artificial, one-sided or unreal. But within, and behind, all these possible social, civic and communal areas for common prayer, there remains the individual, the Muslim or Christian person, in his personal religion. There is surely call in both communities of faith for those who would make their own what they know of their neighbours. To find Lancelot Andrewes and Shāh ʿAbd al-Laṭīf, Francis and Al-Ghazālī, Kierkegaard and Al-Jīlānī, in the same company, rubbing shoulders in an anthology, is to kindle and inform all such personal will to belong more widely in a fellowship of aspiration and of soul. For something of their long separated, and supposedly alien, devotions may pass into the currency of private prayer and, in its measure, dispose the households of distinctive faiths towards a mutual concern with God.

5

If the case is so far made about the single world of one mankind and the compellingly single world of current history, and if it is agreed that we may read in them a call to seek some spiritual crossing of our credal frontiers, then how, and by what authority, and in what terms?

These are daunting questions. It may be well to broach them with another, reflecting, no doubt, the uneasiness some readers will have registered from the start and perhaps have thus far scarcely held in check. Is the God of Islam and the God of Christianity, it will be asked, the same God? If not, and if common prayer is rightly defined as responding to the nature of God, will not such prayer be impossible?

Before we proceed to bare argument here it will be right to give imagination its due place. We do so by recalling two 'neutral' accounts of Muslims at prayer, supposing for the moment that it will be the Christian scepticism about community under God with Muslims that will be the more fortified against persuasion. The first account is from a narrative of seafaring in the waters around Arabia. The Muslim sailors

. . . began the day with prayer. First ablutions, then prayer. The dawn prayer was not communal: each man prayed as best pleased him, having first washed hands and face and feet in water hauled up from the sea. They always stood facing the direction of Mecca . . . stood silent a moment or two in meditation, putting from their minds all unworthy thoughts, and then fell easily and rhythmically into the exercise and words of the set prayers. It was interesting to watch the changes which came over some of their faces. The lines would soften, the flash fade from imperious eyes and whatever there might have been of arrogance, pride, vanity, quite disappear. There was no hypocrisy in those strong faces which looked toward Mecca. It was obvious that their religion was a real and living thing. Their prayers were not simply a formula to be mouthed, but a form of very real communion with a very real god. None of them prayed hurriedly; they always spent a few moments first in silent meditation, in this discard of their worldly thoughts.[1]

In a quite different context, Charles de Foucauld, then a youth-

[1] Alan Villiers: *Sons of Sinbad*, London, 1940, p. 30. The phrasing in the penultimate sentence seems to show that the author is unaware that, for Islam, God can never rightly be spelt with a small 'g' or prefaced with the indefinite article. This in no way impairs the force of his evidence.

ful officer in the French Army in Algeria (*pace* Frantz Fanon),
was first aroused to question his dissolute living and conventional
religion, by the Muslim elements on both sides of combat
abandoning hostilities to fulfil the prayers.

The skirmish continued for a good half hour, with Foucauld
calling at last for fresh ammunition supplies. There was no response
from his own Arabs who had taken cover with the pack animals.
Furious, Foucauld galloped back to read the riot act to his men—
only to find them prostrating themselves in prayer. . . . On the
opposite hillside, too, the firing had stopped. At the risk of being
shot like sitting ducks, the Uled Sidi Sheikh (snipers) had emerged
from cover, turned their backs to the sunset and bowed down to
the east . . . *Allāhu akbar*. A strange silence filled the little wadi, a
stillness that reminded Foucauld of the awesome quiet of Nancy
Cathedral in his boyhood days when he still believed in God. That
silence, in fact, had meant to the boy that he was indeed in the
presence of God. He had laughed at himself since for such mawkish
credulity, but he did not laugh now. These Arabs took God seriously. They had stopped fighting because it was time to pray. . . .
They had exposed themselves to possible massacre to prostrate
themselves before their god, refused to neglect prayer even in the
face of the enemy. . . .[1]

The experience was to remain with Charles de Foucauld as a vital
factor in a conversion to deep Christianity and thus, in turn, to a
heroism of self-expending Christian compassion for Islam, lived
out in the privations of the same Sahara.

Alerted by these witnesses, we return to our question. Is 'the
same God' intended here and in the Christian faith?

The goal, and the terms, of worship, for purposes of a simple
answer, may be likened to what in grammar we know as 'subject'
and 'predicate', the 'theme' and the 'statement'. 'God is great' we
say: or 'men are mortal': or 'knowledge is power'. Or the predi-

---

[1] M. M. Preminger: *The Sands of Tamanrasset: the Story of Charles de
Foucauld*, London, 1961, pp. 55. See also Charles de Foucauld: *Medita-
tions of a Hermit: The Spiritual Writings of Charles de Foucauld*, trans. by
C. Balfour, London, 1961, and R. Voillaume: *Seeds of the Desert*, trans.
by W. Hill, London, 1955. The great French Christian Islamologist,
Louis Massignon, likewise, owed a profound Christian 'conversion' to
Islamic sources.

cates may be verbal instead of adjectival. 'God reigns': 'man dies': 'power corrupts'. Habitually we think of subjects in terms of their predicates. This, of course, is the purpose of predicates. To the degree that they are valid, predicates give us the subject and the subject is expressed in the predicates. When diverse ones are made about one and the same subject, the subject is then differently conceived. But such inconsistencies of predicate are only significant *as differences* if the theme is acknowledged as identical. Without the unity of the subject we cannot change, correct, or even employ, the diverse terms or affirm that some of them are inconsistent.[1]

There is exactly this kind of situation in theology. Islam and Christianity have many common predicates about God—that He is one, creator, lawgiver, provider, ruler, the compassionate, the faithful, the true, the real. There is a single ancestry, too, for many aspects of their doctrine, an ancestry returning to Abraham—a situation to which Hinduism or Buddhism stand in striking contrast. But they have also deeply divergent statements about God, notably in what, for Christianity, has to do with the Father and Shepherd analogies, which involve God with mankind in costly and intimate grace. From these Islam immunizes the Divine majesty and, in its severest mood, insists that you can 'ask Him no questions' and on Him you can 'make no claims'. God is unaffected by human ills and evils and frailties. These are very serious matters in the predicate. They jeopardize the whole Christian understanding of Jesus as God in self-predication. To hold them is to abandon the possibility of the Gospel in any Christian terms.

[1] A simple parallel may help. One may say: 'Princeton is a small, little-known town in the state of Illinois, innocent of university education and having no place in presidential biography.' The reader may at once refute this with indignant insistence that Princeton is in the state of New Jersey and is the seat of a famous university, of which Pres. Woodrow Wilson was once President. The intervention is misled. Princeton, Illinois, is as stated. There are, in fact, both Princetons, indeed half a dozen or more. We cannot disqualify theological predicates, which is what Muslims and Christians often wish to do for each other, unless in fact they 'describe' one God. In this way our very controversies are about a common faith: but, conversely, that common faith is controversial within its unity.

We are thus required to say that God is *not* the 'same' in the two faiths. At first sight, there seems little hope of mutual prayer escaping the vetoes involved in our reciprocal dogmatic disavowals. There can be no mistaking, and certainly no evading, the profound nature of these incompatibilities. No neglect or mitigation of them is here implied or sought. But, necessarily, God, as the theme of these disparities of predicate, is one and the same. If this were not so, the whole issue would dissolve into pluralism, with gods as numerous as there are concepts of him. Neither Christianity nor Islam allows such pluralism. God is one. When they both speak of him, they speak *of him* and there is no duality.

Thus the burden of the disparate predicates persists. Since the one theme of the one God is diversely understood in the statements of doctrine and in the terms of worship our answer to the question whether God in the two faiths is the same God has to be Yes! and No! It cannot honestly be the one answer and not also the other. The duty to say: 'No! they are not identical theologies' belongs *inside* the realization that they relate alike to the one Lord. We are together *under* Him and *in* Him, even when we are diverging *about* Him. The more we long to unify the predicates, each in our own sense (for both faiths are missionary), the more we presume and confess the one reality, and the more need we have of exploring and possessing together the predicates on which we are agreed. These are many and rich. Unless we confess them we lack an honest devotion to those that remain so tragically divided. It is, then, to sloth, or apathy, or pride, not to truth and sincerity, that the task of mutuality will seem impossible. To conclude, we worship the same Lord, in worships informed by significantly similar, as well as sharply discordant, theology.

The further question follows whether this situation admits of unified prayer, in which vocabulary is common and neither party is reduced to a purely passive role in a context which the other dictates. The answer is: Yes! on the ground of the already mutual predicates and within the mercy of the always single Lordship, where, on both counts, there is a large and loyal freedom.

We might test this conclusion by setting the *Fātiḥah*, or opening Surah of the Qur'ān, and the Lord's Prayer, side by side.

In the Name of God, the merciful Lord of mercy. Praise be to God, the Lord of all being, the merciful Lord of mercy, Master of the day of judgment. Thee alone we serve and to Thee alone we come for aid. Guide us in the straight path, the path of those whom Thou hast blessed, not of those against whom there is displeasure, nor of those who go astray.

Our Father, who art in heaven, hallowed be Thy Name: Thy kingdom come: Thy will be done on earth as it is done in heaven. Give us this day our daily bread, and forgive us our trespasses, as we forgive those who trespass against us. And lead us not into temptation, but deliver us from the evil. For Thine is the Kingdom, the power, and the glory, for ever.   Amen.

There are here, to be sure, deep disparities both of phrase and of intention. The opening words 'Our Father' are an immediate obstacle for Muslims, and there is for them a certain perplexity as to how the hallowing of the Name, the coming of the kingdom, and the doing of the will, of God, can well be matters of our intercession.[1] Further, according to many commentators, the distinction made in the final verse of the *Fātiḥah* has reproach of Christians in mind. Though this exegesis is not proven, the formidable Muslim sense of rightness persists as a sanction of aloofness. The difficult situation is reciprocal.

Yet need these facts have the last word? Are they all that should be said? Beyond the first clause, is there anything 'unIslamic' in the Lord's Prayer? Certainly not the conclusion, nor the sense of evil, nor the desire for the will of God, nor the awareness of dependence. 'Forgive us our trespasses' occurs *verbatim* in the Qur'ān. If prejudice in using, or refusing, is surmounted, can there not be a feasible unison of will? Likewise with Christians and the *Fātiḥah*. Its first clause is very close to the *Te Deum Laudamus*: 'Thee, as God, we praise'. Guidance, rectitude, mercy, succour, wrath, lostness—all have Biblical bearings.

---

[1] Taking the point, for example, though not the vehemence, of one of Henry Martyn's 'moonshees'. 'He began with cavilling at the Lord's Prayer . . . particularly: "Hallowed be Thy Name" as if the name of Deity was not absolutely holy'. *Journals and Letters of Henry Martyn*, edited by Samuel Wilberforce, London, 1837, Vol. 2, p. 31.

C

6

Vocabulary, though the realm, is also only the surface, of our problem, and we must turn to a very few acutely sensitive points at which we meet it. To do so we must be able to presuppose a certain mutual forbearance without, in any way, arguing or conceiving this as some sort of 'accommodation' or 'negotiation'. Still less should it be seen as 'sacrifice'. It means, on the contrary, a will to find without compromise of our full selves, the words and phrases which are capable of mutuality of meaning and, within the common will to pray, 'embrace' the other without diminishing the separate intentions of either.

We may perhaps be fortified in this purpose by recalling that, even within a single faith—though with less tension or strangeness—there do coexist a variety of meanings and images of mind. Where Muslims meet, or Christians meet, in their separate communities of customary liturgy and speech, none will say that the words and forms they use carry an equal connotation for them all. Not every Muslim is an Al-Ghazālī, nor every Christian a Francis. Nor, in either camp, are all worshippers unanimous about how they are intending allegory, myth, symbol, creed, confession, reverence or gratitude, or about whether these possess one undifferentiated consistency of meaning for them all, or even from time to time for the same single worshipper, in the flux of his integrity. 'Guide us in the straight path' and 'Deliver us from evil' unify their respective communities of allegiance. But do they not embrace within their meaning a wide range of conscious faith and aspiration, all of it sincere, from the mundane to the sublime?

The mosque is known in Islam as 'the gatherer'. There, and in the Christian 'assembly', men privately differ within the public unity. Otherwise, there would be no need for the Christian liturgy, for example, to use those phrases about One 'to Whom all hearts are open, all desires known, and from Whom no secrets are hid'. All corporate worship resembles an arch, under which a diversity of folk and needs and yearnings can shelter, reaching Godward from where they stand within it. Language, of itself, can never ensure sincerity, but neither can it ever deny or exclude it. Words in prayer, within or beyond one faith-community, are never more than the opportunity of the soul, the voice of our intention. Truly we must care for them scrupulously. But it is we who give them reality and they must be seen as spaces, not prisons, for our hearts.

Interior divergencies of will and desire are vitally to be distinguished, of course, from coexistence in exterior relationships. But the problems are not dissimilar, if only we are persuaded that there exists a sufficient consensus of conviction—the sort of limited but significant consensus which this collection of prayers is believed to demonstrate, and demonstrate compellingly enough both to furnish and inspire some further attainment of its evident community of mind.

In that concern, each faith will be called upon for some readiness to forgo, without embarrassment or compromise, precious elements of its own heritage which are second nature to it. Muslims, for example, will find here no *Taṣliyah*, no salutation of Muhammad, no greeting of his 'Companions', and no petition about 'dying a Muslim'. These cannot be sincerely shared by Christians. This is not to say that Christians, by this inability, mean to depreciate Muhammad, or that they do not deeply recognize the intensity of Islamic assurance about him and the Muslims' concern for his due acceptance. But, in this context of mutual praying, these questions are in suspension—not in indifference or neglect, but in suspension, in the sense that they do not have to be answered within the terms of the enterprise in hand. It is recognized that a devotional relationship towards God without the explicit conjuncture of the second half of the *Shahādah*, or confession of faith, is an exacting silence for Muslims.

There is, likewise, a large 'silence' here for the Christian also. Prayers do not begin or end with terms that Muslims cannot employ. The words 'Father, Son and Holy Spirit', and the phrase 'through Jesus Christ our Lord', are absent from the pages that follow. There will be many Christians who will honestly decline ever to pray without these words, just as there will be Muslims unable to forgo their equally crucial language about Muhammad. For such consciences there must be due honour and understanding. Plainly, for these, in either community, the venture of mutual prayer is precluded. It will be enough if they are ready at least to keep their decision constantly under review and hold their bolder colleagues in their hearts. But need fidelity always and only cast the die this way? Must there not be an equal freedom for those who sense an honest possibility of a partial rendezvous of praise and petition? If so, they will owe it to their communities to interpret the principles of their decision and their communities will owe that loyalty a careful understanding.

7

There are duties here which can only be fully undertaken from within. Only Muslims can finally determine the prayer limits of Islam, though the quality of Christian relationship may well help or hinder their decisions. On the Christian side, the matter turns, essentially, on the question whether prayer is 'Christian' without the explicit conclusion: '. . . through Jesus Christ our Lord'. The Lord's Prayer itself, it is true, does not conclude in this way. Nor is there record, for example, that the prayers of Lydia and others at Philippi when Paul joined them (Acts 16:13–14), could yet have done so. But it must also be agreed that the phrase becomes normal and universal at a very early point in the Church. Its theological meaning is that we come to God on the ground of his nature, of his Name and that, for Christians, his nature and his Name are assured to us in the life and ministry and passion of Jesus as the Christ. We also mean that all we ask and seek is to be desired, interpreted and told in consistency with 'the mind of Christ', and in the context of his self-offering in redemptive love. For Christians, as Paul writes in the Second Epistle to the Corinthians, Christ is 'the Amen', and in him 'all the pledges of God' find their fulfilment. He is the criterion and the ground on which the Christian can truly say: '*So* be it.'

The clause 'through Jesus Christ our Lord' is not, then, an arbitrary formula, a talisman, present only when it is verbally uttered, or sure only where it is vocalized. It is rightly understood as synonymous with the equivalent, and even prior, phrase: 'for the sake of Thy Name', or 'according to Thy will and glory'. These, with Amen, are phrases with positive significance for Muslims. To pray in the Divine Name is implicitly to pray 'in Christ', as far as the inwardness of Christians is concerned. Using it, without inward loss, Christians defer to the exigencies of a common vocabulary, when they adopt the form of words that grounds itself simply on the Divine Name. There is always the possibility in the Spirit, that agreement of terms, with disparity of content but sincerity of heart, may grow and converge into larger relevance. It was so when New Testament writers made Greek terms their own which purists or diehards insisted were unwarranted or dubious. Not seldom has ambiguity, patiently allowed, proved to be the space where truth has been more truthfully possessed and souls therein enlarged.

But we must refuse the accusation which takes these accepted, if normally unacceptable, limitations of vocabulary as somehow compromise. Risks there are, undoubtedly, but these are inseparable from any living theology and to be without them is to be imprisoned. It may be interesting here to recollect that we are involved in the reverse direction of an old issue in the primitive Church. Devotion, not simply 'in the name of Jesus Christ our Lord' but to 'Jesus' without express reference to 'God' or 'the Father', and also prayer to Jesus as God, grew among the first Christians by a natural instinct of the heart. It even began with Stephen at his martyrdom (Acts 7:59). Such usage was, in fact, a proper element in the awareness of the Incarnation and, as a devotional instinct, it played a considerable part in the urge to, and the shaping of, a right theology. But, at the same time, it properly aroused a countering concern lest it obscure or preclude that right theology, by somehow disallowing, in unintended implication, the God of the Incarnation in the very eagerness that confessed the Incarnation of God. Hence the need to discipline and curb the habit of prayer to Christ for the truer acknowledgement of God in Christ.[1] Something of the liturgical legacy of this

---

[1] This writer has made some attempt, in simple terms, to make the necessary theological alertness here plain in *The Call of the Minaret*, New York and London, 1956, pp. 314–16.

issue remains, as Maurice Wiles observes, in the structure of the great hymn: *Gloria in excelsis Deo*, where the praise of God and of the Christ blend into one sequence.[1] We need not be surprised then if some of those who were criticized for a Christly devotion inquired: 'Why? What evil am I doing glorifying Christ?'[2] In our present argument we are asking: 'Why are we suspect for glorifying the Divine Name?'

If this readiness for the more inclusive formula were to be seen by the dubious as a retreat from Christology, the answer would be twofold. There is, firstly, the sufficient reason of the will to spiritual relationship beyond the Church. Secondly, there is the fact that the whole, i.e. the Divine Name, always has the whole within it, whether or not its content is explicitly denoted in the way that Christians believe is the case when we say: 'Blessed be God, the Father of our Lord Jesus Christ.' To have said: 'Blessed be God', as a Christian, is to have said the whole. We have not then hallowed God, so to speak, in only part of himself: we have rejoiced in *all* that the mention of God enfolds in Christian conviction. The full measure of that Divinity abides in the unfailing Christological self-expression—a reality about which we need have no nervous fear, as if it were insecure without our words.

This, of course, is not to deny the necessity of the *confessio fidei* in its own interior place, where, as we have said, it will remain. But it *is* to see that confession alive to the ventures it owes outside itself. If some in the early Church needed to bring their Christ-devotion more carefully 'into God', are there not some in the contemporary Church who need to reach out more readily from their Christology 'into God'? This will in no way mean leaving it behind. It is, rather, proceeding upon it (upon the conviction of God self-predicated in Christ) more confidently, by virtue of the very will to converse with those whose confession of God excludes that conviction. The way, surely, is not to see their persuasion of God as wanting and reject it, but as operative and engage with it. As an expectant, rather than simply a doctrinaire, position, will not this be more loyal to the ever-patient Christ,

---

[1] In *The Making of Christian Doctrine*, Cambridge, 1967, p. 76.
[2] *Ibid.*, p. 71, in the example of Noetus, quoted from Hippolytus.

the Christ who stands and knocks? Do we primarily want a theology that 'secures' God or that 'seeks' men?

The Christian need not doubt that Christ gathers into his intercession, with us and through us, that which lacks the explicit ascription of his name. For the great metaphors about God in Christ have to do with risk and venture and initiative, not with immunity and reservation. According to Paul, in the Epistle to the Philippians (2:5–11), the concern of the Christ is not with his 'reputation', but with the Divine will. His purpose is not first to be duly recognized but duly to redeem. The familiar passage about not counting equality with God a status to be held tight and clutched,[1] a dignity whose essence is to be preserved, sets a quality of self-expenditure at the very heart of the Christian faith about the nature of love and of God. Yet we are so often manoeuvred into a position where, controversially, we are jealously defending and 'securing' the very status of Sonship which, in fact, consists in the very antithesis of such 'security'. Christians must pause over a zeal that defends a status and yet sees no calling to imitate its secret, or has only a Christology of assertion with which to affirm the Christ of self-limitation.

Since we have appealed to this passage and its supreme lesson about majesty fulfilled in *kenosis* or self-giving, it is only fair to remember how it concludes:

Wherefore God also has highly exalted him and given him the name that is above every name: that in the name of Jesus every knee should bow . . . and that every tongue should confess that Jesus Christ is Lord. . . .

How, it must be asked, is this triumphant conclusion as to the Lordship of Jesus the Christ to be reconciled with our willingness, in the foregoing, to pray without the explicit occurrence of his name and with those who, for all their reverent recognition of his prophethood and honour, stop firmly short of acknowledging that 'he is Lord'?

The answer, in part, lies in taking this great New Testament passage as the due form of Christian expectancy within the

[1] There is no doubt that the sense of this crucial passage is caught in the modern notion of 'status' as 'self-conserving'.

representative drama of the Messiah. There is this unqualified worth in the redemptive achievement of Christly suffering, by which universal mankind is known to be included, without exception or remainder, in an obligation of recognition and surrender. That which has at its heart the one inclusive secret of the conquest of evil has, by that very virtue, the right to un-reserving and unbounded empire.

It cannot be too often emphasized that the New Testament faith hinges decisively on the identification, in Jesus crucified, of that realized Messiahship which is the justification of God, the effective Divine response to the wilfulness of human history and the whole wrongness of the world. In Messiah-Jesus faith recognizes the action of God for humanity, at once vindicating the Divine sovereignty, retrieving the thwarted creation and 'saving lost mankind'. In the double sense of Jesus as 'Christ' and as 'Lord'—the one by the fact of the other—the Gospel brings together the characteristic themes of Old Testament religion, on the one hand, and of Greek wisdom on the other. Here in Christ is, at once, 'the power and the wisdom of God'.

Paul, in Philippians, sees this history of Messiah's humiliation and victory, his patience, passion and glory, as the enactment in reverse of that honour and dishonour, high calling and deep tragedy, which is the story of man, of 'Adam', of the race in its destiny and disorder. The faithful 'Son of Man' brings back what fallen man had forfeited and opens the kingdom of heaven for the barred gates of Eden. In the paradigm of Messiah's fidelity man's inner falsehood is made whole on the condition of a vital faith. This, in familiar summary, is the living meaning of the Christ, the Jesus who is Lord, as it is declared in 'the word of the Gospel'.

Hence, here in Philippians and always, it becomes the pattern of the Christian calling. 'Let this mind be in you.' The redeemed must be the redeeming: the Messiah will energize Messianic community to perpetuate his saving secret and to follow the pattern of his humility. Paul and the other New Testament writers are always both doctrinal and moral in their concern. The great celebration of the Christ in Philippians 2 ends with the demand for obedience and the implementing, the 'working out', of the grace of Christ—and that, even apprehensively, lest one should fail it.

Such, in brief, is the inner, positive meaning of a most definitive passage in Christian Scripture. It must be taken in the full tide of its own ardour and assurance. It would be foreign to its import, and false to its magnificent poetry, to see in it a nervous verdict against other religions. Its whole apprehension is inward, lest Christians impede its authority in their own lives. The New Testament is not working out here a philosophy of relationship with Buddhism, Hinduism, or Islam. It is wholly unaware of them. Its positive confidence is that anywhere, everywhere, in all the corners of the earth and to the end of time, there is in the suffering, risen Christ the clue to man's salvation. Jesus is affirmed to be the one in whom history must and will identify its master and recognize its true glory. And such recognition will rightly command every soul of man, since the humanity is one for which this Lordship holds. This is what the passage says. Let us not withdraw it simply into eschatology; for it is present ethics also. But let us not divert its supreme positive, both for there and then and here and now, into an argument tending to isolation from those who, for whatever reasons—not all of them perverse and some of them compulsive—withhold their conviction or assent. We cannot paraphrase Paul as saying: '. . . that without the name of Jesus no knee should ever bow', or human frame prostrate. We must not reverse the agonized father in the Gospel and think to say: 'Lord, we believe, exclude Thou their unbelief.'

There are, no doubt, aspects of this theme of universal claim and actual diversity which would be relevant, if this were an essay on the philosophy of religion and not simply an introduction to the prayers of two adjacent faiths. But if it were, the clue probably lies in some sense of the interior validity of belief which, in its inwardness, does not disqualify, and is not disqualified by, the outside 'quarrel' of contrasted or divergent systems. These, in their turn, have a certain interior immunity from the reach of tenets which, likewise, assess or controvert them from without. To say this is neither to argue the transcendental unity of all religions, nor yet to turn them into closed circuits, immune from relationships of kinship or repulsion. For our present purposes,

it will be well to hold together the positive inward commitment
and the open outward reach, 'with reverence and godly fear', and
to ask this of Muslims and Christians alike.

There is, perhaps, occasion in this context to take up the query
some may wish to press about the over-all use of the title-phrase
'Alive to God' in a comprehensive sense, when it is, of course,
borrowed from a closely argued passage of Paul, in a distinctively
Christian way. He called upon his readers, Christians in Rome,
to 'reckon themselves dead indeed unto sin, but alive to God
through Jesus Christ'. His plea falls squarely within a piece of
deeply Christian thinking, for which the death and resurrection
of Christ is received as an active parable of the death and new life
of the disciple also, the death, that is, of the old, self-centred
nature and a new aliveness to God in a transformed personality.
This theme recurs throughout the Christian Scriptures. The
Christ-event is both history and experience. A 'Christ mysticism',
as some outsiders call it, finds the going down and the rising up
of Christ in his humiliation and victory a 'mystery' enacted also
within the soul, in the critical moral meaning of faith. Baptism
embodies the symbolism, as the sacrament of incorporation into
Christ, signing men 'with the sign of the Cross' to claim them for
a revolutionary goodness. Christianity will always be concerned
to hold this meaning clear, *ut non evacuetur crux Christi*. Thus,
for example, the ancient prayer of Easter Sunday asks 'that, as
by thy special grace preceding us, thou dost put into our minds
good desires, so by thy continual help we may bring the same to
good effect'—a petition that, aside from this understanding, might
seem a very modest celebration of the Resurrection!

There is, then, no doubt what the phrase we have borrowed
means in Paul's terms. But are we, therefore, to think that, apart
from this sense of being 'in Christ', there is no aliveness before
God, no vitality of worship, no awareness of wonder, fear or
thankfulness? 'I endeavoured to think how he [Paul] would act
in my situation', Henry Martyn once wrote.[1] It is certainly hard
to conjecture how the great convert of Damascus would have
reckoned with the great other conversion of Damascus itself six

[1] Quoted from *Memoir of Henry Martyn*, by John Sargent, London,
1816, p. 107.

centuries later. There was, at any rate, one circumstance they shared. 'Look! he prays' was the arresting comment about the former, in the immediate sequel to his crisis of belief. And prayer was from the beginning the hallmark of the latter, the sign and token of the sway of Islam.

Having safeguarded the Christian context of Paul's words 'alive to God', as they stand in the Epistle to the Romans 6:11, we may surely allow them a currency in wider, if also in some sense narrower, terms. This is the more right at a time in the secular sphere where 'a-dying' seems a more current term than 'alive' when worship and its themes are spoken of. For when we think that 'God is dead' it is rather that we are not alive.

8

This very theme of vitality and 'coming alive' is well calculated to serve our transition to the Islamic assessments of what we have here in view. For Islam sees itself as, truly, the ultimate form of alertness to God, informed by a final revelation and bringing to a climax the primal reality of religion. It is the properly human worship of God, here properly exalted and enthroned. Nowhere, Muslims believe, is the religious meaning of God over man and of man under God more authentically defined, illuminated and enabled. And in this vital awareness of God man truly comes alive. For here is the true dynamism of belief.

It was by way of birth . . .
That you came into this dimensional world:
The first birth is by constraint, the second by choice: . . .
For the first is a seeking, the second a finding . . .
A child is born through the rending of the womb;
A man is born through the rending of the world.
The call to prayer signalizes both kinds of birth,
The first is uttered by the lips, the second of the very soul.[1]

[1] Muḥammad Iqbāl: *Jāvīd Nāmā*, trans. by A. J. Arberry, London, 1966, lines 279, 80, 85, 88, 93–6.

Ḥayya is the arousing initial word in that call to prayer, repeated many times a day by the muezzin. 'Come ye unto worship: come ye unto the good.' It is an imperative from the root verb, to live, to come alive. At the dawn, the muezzin joins the rising out of sleep to the better awakening unto God.

The response of Muslims to this call of Islam makes for an exclusively Islamic solidarity. It means an experience of uniqueness at least as insistent as any other religious allegiance. There are reasons in Islam for a no less emphatic dissociation from what is not Islam as those we have been pondering in Christianity—different reasons, it is true, but no less tenacious and assertive. Islam does not confess a central mystery of Incarnation nor a singular drama of redemption. But it sees its vital belief in the Divine unity and its witness to the final prophethood of Muḥammad as meaning a custodianship of truth separating Islam from all earlier, partial or compromised systems. It has in its own keeping the criterion by which it is validated and all else is judged.

Its Pillars, as they are called, of cultic expression all share this sacrosanct character with the doctrine to which they belong. Prayer, or *Ṣalāt*, the first of them after the *Shahādah* or *confessio fidei* itself, is, in its specific ritual shape, the given, undeviating, undeviated obligation. Its non-observance, said the theologians, indicated the non-recognition of the faith of which it was the mandatory evidence. *Īmān*, or belief, had its corollary in *Dīn*, or religious acts. To fail or distort the latter was to belie the former. Anything, therefore, that seems to involve in any way the unchanging form and duty of Islamic *Ṣalāt* impugns the whole nature of Islamic obligation both as to creed and conduct.

So vigilant and vigorous is this understanding of ritual prayer that, from time to time, even inward and complementary forms of prayer in Islam have been suspect in some quarters, especially when they led to the celebration of the saints of Islam or, for some purists, the celebration of Muḥammad himself. The strictures, for example, of the Wahhābis in this field are well known. However, extra-ritual prayer, or *Duʿāʾ*, has a long and undeniable place in Muslim piety and it is broadly from this realm that the present collection is drawn. In the best hands *Duʿāʾ* stays very closely with the temper and the themes of *Ṣalāt* and with the

Fātiḥah, which, it can be claimed, is central to both. *Duʿāʾ*, however, admits of free, personal patterns, a closer tie with the immediate preoccupations of daily life and a more explicit self-examination. Though it has often found liturgical forms among the Ṣūfī Muslims, it has a greater spontaneity of language and content than *Ṣalāt*, by its very nature, admits. Its honoured place in the wealth of Islamic devotion justifies a general appeal to it as giving warrant to a will in Islam for a community of spirituality beyond the 'ecclesiastical' community of *Ṣalāt* in Islam or of Islam within *Ṣalāt*.[1] If Muslims alone are truly 'bowers before God' (the root sense of *Ṣalāt*) Muslims *and* others may be 'callers upon Him' (the root sense of *Duʿāʾ*). This arguably gives Christians their opportunity without any trespass upon the exclusivity of the right prostration, always assuming, of course, that these extra canonical acts of prayer are not repugnant to the temper of *Ṣalāt*. It is believed that everything here meets that condition.

We still confront, however, many other sources of Muslim unease about prayer with non-Muslims. Can you supersede what is inferior and yet also see it as a partner? But can there be a finalizing faith without at least some ambivalence in the relationship? For, if the progression occurs, it cannot only be negative. In the inevitable reflection of this ambivalence in the Qurʾān one thing at all events is clear. It is that, historically, the Qurʾān shows a significant cognizance of Christian worship—significant enough to afford, in all likelihood, a precious theological metaphor.

In a well-known passage from the Surah of Light (Surah 24:35–37), the light of God is likened to

... a lamp in a glass (fed by the oil of the olive and set) in houses God has permitted to be established, where His Name is commemorated and men, whom neither trading nor transacting diverts from the remembrance of God, celebrate His praises, morning and evening, performing the prayer and bringing the alms ...

[1] Maybe 'ecclesiastical' is an incongruous adjective to employ here. It is, however, strictly accurate, in that those who pray in Islam are 'called out' of their preoccupations (not their homes, save on Fridays at noon, since prayer is not necessarily mosque-centred) into a recognizable community engaged in its identifying duty by a common, periodic summons.

in fear of the last day. While the concluding phrases have the characteristically Islamic ritual (*Ṣalāt* and *Zakāt*) in mind, can there be serious doubt that in the background of the metaphor, with its careful detail, is Christian monasticism and perhaps even the sanctuary lamp of Holy Communion? At least we may say that here are associations clear enough to be Christian, if not exclusively or actually so, and that they belong with the Qur'ān's own theology of worship in a most telling way. Even a tentative case suffices for our cause.

Central to Islam is a deep reverence for Jesus as teacher and prophet, second only to Muḥammad and uniquely esteemed as 'God's spirit'. While the sense in which Christianity receives and confesses him is repeatedly repudiated as deplorable, there are areas of Jesus' word and example that are unaffected by this conflict. His teaching about prayer and his practice of it—aside from the address of God as 'Father' and the inward counterpart of that address in 'Sonship'—fall within the positive Muslim acknowledgement of Jesus, though the Qur'ān records little detail of them. There are interesting Quranic echoes of the sayings of Jesus, all of which bear upon our hope. Themes from the Sermon on the Mount, for example, may be discerned in the following: 'Call upon your Lord with humble entreaty in secret. . . . Remember your Lord in your soul humbly and in secret, not being loud in speech' (Surah 7:55 and 205): 'Forgive us our trespasses . . .' (Surah 3:16 and 193): '. . . those who join what God has commanded shall be joined . . . and who turn back evil with good' (Surah 13:21–22). A familiar metaphor of the New Testament recurs, with precisely the same question as to whether it is a 'camel' or a 'cable' that is meant: 'Those who belie our signs and set themselves up proudly against them, the gates of heaven will not be open to them, nor will they enter the garden, until the camel shall pass through the eye of the needle' (Surah 7:40).

Penetrating the traditions of Muslim piety we find, as in this anthology, many traces of Christian ethics and of the moral concerns which the New Testament Epistles learned and enjoined from 'the obedience of Christ'. Jalāl al-Dīn Rūmī, for example, speaks the same language as the parable of the last judgement, as it occurs in the Gospel according to Matthew (25:30 f.). God is to be recognized in the need of the hungry and there is an inwardness about true religion. There is no valid occasion, because of the deep contention about Jesus the Lord, to justify either Muslims or Christians precluding from the other such obedience to Jesus the teacher as may be within the reach of both.

If we insist on the enmities, we shall have to reproach the God who disregards them. There is a question in the *Gulistān* of Saʿdī which runs:

> O bountiful One, who from Thy invisible treasury
> Suppliest the Guebre and the Christian with food,
> How could'st Thou disappoint Thy friends,
> Whilst having regard for Thy enemies?[1]

We cannot have it both ways. If 'they' are enemies they are not abandoned and if 'we' are God's friends we are not exclusively befriended. Either God is wrong about an openness to compassion which does not first demand the right credentials, or we are wrong in the closedness that requires them.

There is much else in Islam to indicate that Saʿdī's question has its answer. The diversity of men is by the Divine will and to every nation a prophet is sent. Even different worships are Divinely appointed among different peoples (Surah 22:67). While the Qur'ān affirms their culmination in, and interpretation according to, Islam, that very conviction casts a backward relevance over what they mean and do. The doctrine of finality involves the Muslim in concern with what has been preparatory. On the most obdurate view of the Islamic ultimacy, supersession cannot rightly be seen as entire repudiation. It means a definitive relationship to what is in measure incorporated from the past. If only on this rigorous score, Islam has inner integrity in any converse with Christianity.

In this connection, its time-position after its monotheistic predecessors in no way disengages it from elements which they anticipated. It is easy, of course, in the before-and-after sequence,

---

[1] *The Gulistan, or Rose Garden of Saʿdi*, trans. by Edward Rehatsek, London, 1964, p. 57. The Guebre is the Zoroastrian.

to note relationships and see them as supersession. It is no less important, in the after-and-before direction, to discern relationships and see them determining precedents fit to be abiding. In this kind of situation, mere chronology has no place. The core of the New Testament, it may be said, is already 'islamic' in the issues it faces and 'un-islamic' in the decisions it takes, especially Gethsemane as its definitive event. But, by the same token, it is also deeply islamic in its concerns to which those decisions belong —the sovereignty of God, the universality of mercy, the correction of evil, the release of thanksgiving and the claims of eternity.

These can perhaps be focused here into the dethronement of idolatry. There is no more splendid, and effective, liberation of idolaters from their futility and fear than New Testament religion. 'You turned to God from idols, to serve the living and true God', wrote Paul to the Thessalonians. Surely here, for all the divergencies of diagnosis and remedy, is a cause for Muslim openness of heart? For Islam is committed to antipathy for all *Shirk*, to *jihād* against all false worship, and to the reversal of all non-*islām*. The essence of non-*islām* is the idol power, the false absolute, the disowning of God.[1] Is it not clear that all Christianity, and the Christian prayers herewith, have to do, decisively and devotedly, with this supremely islamic concern that 'God may be all in all'? If we cannot be well together on the ground of Islam, can we not be found together at least in common struggle against non-*islām*, against all that is insubordinate to the will, the mercy and the rule of God?

Our intercessions, at any rate, even where they stay apart, must necessarily relate to many of the same evils—pride, greed, malice, hate, sloth, Belial, Mammon, Mars, Venus, sin and sins, no doubt divergently understood in our ethical systems but certainly the same in our human predicament and perversity.

---

[1] The argument here, of course, turns on the simple fact that Islam is both the name of an historical religion and a simple, common noun meaning the effective acknowledgement of God.

9

'A burning fire', as the proverb says, 'does not kindle moist wood.' Are our fuels ready for kindling? This anthology hopes to confirm an affirmative answer. With these underlying issues for the theologies of either faith thus far reviewed, go many implicit feelings inseparable from living devotion. What is to be said about the whole feel and atmosphere of prayer, of vocabulary—not primarily now as a theological question but as an emotional possession? The invocation, the ascription, the emphases, nuances, and silences, are all part of a psychology of prayer which many will consider insuperably different. Even if we can align them intellectually, can we forgo and forbear with them spiritually? Prayer is a poetry of the soul, and poems are inherently *within* their own matrix of word, music, tradition, and temper. To qualify in meeting do we not disqualify in meaning?

Before attempting any answer here, let us face the alternative to which some readers may have been tending in their reactions as they read. Granted that there is need of common action in society, common openness of spirit, common concern in the world, can we not better find these by occasional attendance at acts of worship that are still wholly under the aegis of one, or of the other, faith? Christians may sometimes be present in the mosque and Muslims in the church. We might even hold their pulpits open for certain limited themes of feasible exhortation or counsel, when public occasion requires. Do we not already in courtesy attend weddings, funerals, or memorial services in each other's religious frames of reference and of doctrine? Do we not exchange greetings beyond our faith-communities, when there is a festival or an ʿīd which seems, somehow, to belong socially to both communities? Is it not more safe and prudent to bring our presence into the others' prayers, with sympathy and silence, rather than venture into the difficult world of somehow 'neutralized' language and form? Will there not be less danger of hypocrisy and misconception this way? Are there really any, in either camp, who are ready for more?

These considerations need to be respected. Such suggestions

D

can be contributory. They are better than disdain, or aloofness, or deadness to God. In some situations they may be more viable and feasible than any other way. But as a final definition of either hope or duty, or as an ultimate intention, they are open to one overriding objection. Unless we are tackling the problems of mutuality as we have been exploring them here, all such participation will be that of 'passengers' being 'conveyed', at worst merely physically present for the sake of a unity they do not seek, at best spiritually inarticulate in a unity they do not find. And prayer is never physically achieved and never spiritually dormant. Mere presence may show a will to prayer but a will to prayer is never merely shown. If it is meant as a satisfactory goal, the more prudent, and certainly the more easy, suggestion must be rejected. We are returned to our more fundamental problems, but with a sense that precisely because they are still problems they are authentic.

One reassuring factor here is the degree to which a kindred shape already characterizes Christian and Muslim forms in Collect and *Du'ā'*. The latter is often almost wholly invocatory: it is, literally, a 'calling upon God'. It proceeds upon the Quranic injunction: 'God's are the most excellent Names, so call upon Him by them' (Surah 7:180), with its double sense of ascribing and addressing at the same time. It consists, then, simply in the recital, as being also the plea, of the Names. The petition is thus entirely implicit. 'O Thou Opener' suffices as a prayer to God about a new year, or a new ledger, or a new dwelling. One does not need to indicate in further words what it will take for God to be himself in and for the situation out of which the invocation cries. The intention of the faith that prays is wholly focused in the kindly answerability of God to his Names.

To many Christian observers this has seemed an unfortunate reluctance to be really 'asking', a lack, as it were, of the assurance which is truly petitionary with trustful detail and a baring of the heart. For the Muslim, however, there is a deference and a dignity in this simplicity, from which the wordy Christian may take a salutary lesson. Examples are many in the text below. The Christian instinct to bring one's sense of the mercy and power of God into conscious relation with the living scene, and even to venture, like Abraham, a dialogue with God about the meaning of his will, need not be disconcerted. Nor need economy of words be taken as a criterion of all that prayer entails.

The metaphors of theology no doubt have their effect here, whether those of Fatherhood or those of Lordship. But is it not possible that a patient openness of either to the other may enlarge and liberate what they are in their interior and customary character? Many ancient Christian collects have, in their chaste and studied language, the same invocatory directness that Islam condenses into the *du'ā'* of a Name. The theme of their petition is directly linked with the attribute noted, for thanksgiving, in their prelude.

O Lord, from whom all good things do come, grant to us thy humble servants that by thy holy inspiration we may think those things that be good. . . .

O God, whose nature and property is ever to have mercy and to forgive . . . let the pitifulness of thy great mercy loose us. . . .

These, and many others, are in their form and pattern, remarkably akin to the Muslim sense that praise and petition are really one. Is there not a kinship and a co-education in this situation?

Similarly, there may be mutual learning in the contrasted postures in which we may both be saying: 'Thy will be done', or 'So be it'. The *Amen* of all prayer contains a hidden, or not so hidden, diversity. Do we intend: 'Thy will be accepted' simply; or 'Thy will be achieved'? Are we submissive to what we cannot change, or resolute, even angry, about what we must? The petition surely belongs with a revolutionary as well as with a mourner. It is ardent for righteousness as well as acquiescent in sorrow. In either case, we need a steady vigilance about how we understand the interrelation of God's will and men's. Is there not a chance that, in the exacting issues of this ancient question, we may more truly belong with what we pray because we do not isolate the praying?

Nor need we at all imagine that Muslim praying is necessarily that of resignation and static submission. On the contrary, the Qur'ān may be freely invoked to sustain a dynamic vitalism which sees the Divine will as turning upon a human energy of purpose as its vehicle. Islam stands squarely in the Biblical tradition of God active in history and of history as the arena of personal significance, struggle, tragedy, judgement, and decision, not of abstraction and mere intellection. God is the God of Abraham, of Moses, of the prophets, of the *Hijrah* and of the *Ummah*, the community of the God-fearers, not of the philosophers and theorists. The interpretation of prayer urged in the poetry and lectures of Muḥammad Iqbāl is in this sense representative, novel as some of his emphases undoubtedly were. He is wholly committed to a vigorous activism as the proper counterpart of Divine faith.

He writes:

Prayer as a means of spiritual illumination is a normal, vital act, by which the little island of our personality suddenly discovers its situation in a larger whole of life.

After noting that congregationality in prayer incorporates the person in the human community, he interprets the postures of Islamic prayer as symbolizing 'both affirmation and negation', so that the self

. . . in the very moment of negation . . . discovers its own worth and justification as a dynamic factor in the life of the universe.[1]

There is, arguably, in the different postures and convictions of Christian prayer the double sense of penitence, of a self being negated in contrition, and of discipleship and the undertaking of the Divine will.

> O that a man might arise in me
> That the man I am might cease to be.

In this sense, however contrasted, prayers have a potential kinship, reinforced by several other related themes to be found side by side in the pages below. There is, not least of them, the deep Muslim Christian centrality of gratitude as, in a way, the real touchstone of belief. *Shukr*, or thankfulness, is opposed to *kufr*, or unbelief, in the Qur'ān. The latter is an inclusive term and denotes the false relationship men have with the God they

---

[1] *The Reconstruction of Religious Thought in Islam*, Lahore, 1930, pp. 91 and 93.

deny and ignore. *Kufr* is both in one: it is the essential a-theism, or no-God-ness, which does not doubt wistfully (an always redeemable case), but dismisses gracelessly. The Qur'ān is often impressed with this gracelessness of men: 'Most of them do not give thanks' (Surahs 2:243; 10:60; 12:38; 27:73; 40:61, etc.).

Such instinct to understand faith in terms of gratitude opens wide doors of relationship. For where dogmatic tests would have to disown and exclude, deep, undisputed springs of wonder and thanksgiving may well be found to veto those vetoes and to indicate that there is community beyond the frontiers of dogma. To assert the Divinity of Christ puts a Christian out of Muslim acceptance. But what, if synonymously with that confession, we also sing: 'Thanks be unto God for His unspeakable gift'? The gratitude at least may begin to qualify for recognition.

So, at least, it is that praise may still unite where dogma requires to scrutinize. The one need not always wait for the other. And when it does, many, though not all, the themes of praise will be seen to be in tune. The Bible and the Qur'ān are full of the splendour and the mystery of the universe, the fidelities of nature, the strange entrustments of pregnancy and harvest, the flux of winds and seas, the path of ships, the force of storm and fire, and all the pageantry of hills, and wells, and tribes, and creatures 'great and small'. There is, wide and unmistakable, a single field of common praise, tuning man's instruments of reverence in the chorus of grateful dependence and received significance. For all these are 'the signs of God', ministering the Divine power and mercy to 'a people that understand'.

The mercies of God in the different fields of prophet and Messiah, of revelation and Scriptures and their institutional issue into faiths—in dispute and contention as these are—still have mutual features we must be careful not to miss. The rule of God, the instrumentality of men, the moral of history, the care of time, the reckoning with death, are among them. The diagnosis of sin, despite the different law, has elements in common, especially if we keep in mind the clue, above, about ingratitude.[1]

---

[1] As R. Bultmann observes: 'Self-assertion can be understood as guilt only if it can be understood as ingratitude.' *Kerugma and Myth*, edited by H. W. Bartsh, trans. by R. H. Fuller, London, 1953, p. 31.

The prayers of penitence in this collection are no less proof of community than those of praise. The theme of forgiveness is vital in Islam. There *is* a disparity—perhaps wider here than anywhere among the things that separate. But there are present many of the same awarenesses. It is 'the good things', says the Qur'ān, 'which outweigh (or 'rout') the evil things' (Surah 11:113). The saying may simply be a maxim about rewards. But with the call to patience in the context, it may be more than a hint of the principle that goodness has the power of outstaying the worst that evil can do and so of undoing and transmuting its authority. All forgiveness must explore this mystery. For it repays 'with what is fairer . . .' (Surahs 23:96; 41:34, etc.), and so knows from within the travail that undoes the evil. 'In detesting hatred', wrote Ionesco, 'I become full of hatred myself and start playing hatred's game'.[1] So 'what is fairer' has to resist and redeem together. Wrong is not saved without condemnation, nor yet by it. And 'God knows what we conceal in our hearts'.

It is probably safer to leave these matters here with hints rather than with argument. For they emerge better in the living context of learning to pray, where we are beyond hypocrisy in the sense that we detect how it still pursues us. Humility is a virtue much praised by proud men, and evil much debated by unforgiving ones. We know better when we proceed. May not the experience be in measure mutual in the company of our several masters in the art of prayer? Only so shall we, in Ezra Pound's phrase, 'maintain antisepsis'—moral antisepsis in the distracted human world and in the contagion of our innermost souls.

10

These considerations must also be our reply to the accusation that is, perhaps, preparing, especially from the Christian side, that this alignment of diverse prayers is too easy and eclectic, that it leaves out all inconvenient incompatibles and, so doing, main-

[1] *Notes and Counter Notes*, trans. by D. Watson, London, 1964, p. 167.

tains a far too sanguine, even superficial, idea of human religious-
ness and in no way reckons with the guilt and perversity of piety
itself.

On the first count, the anthology has to be its own evidence.
All selection is arbitrary and may owe as much to ignorance as to
choice. But at least it is genuine and has, in a sense, gathered itself
by its own qualities, which had simply to be identified. No one
denies that it would have been possible to compile a totally
discordant collection of Christian/Muslim sentiments, a kind of
cacophony of denunciation, a mutual malediction. The resources
exist in history. There are spectres still quick of hearing and ready
for recall. But to silence them is no conspiracy or fraud. Nor, when
they are silenced, is there only silence. There may then be heard
in authenticity the concordant things with which, here, we have
to do.

On the second count, there is no wise denial of the temptations
of religion. Prayers have no exemption from the deceptiveness of
man. But immunity is not to be found by staying only with the
familiar, nor is sincerity the more imperilled by the unfamiliar.
The answer to the deceits of religious man is not to find them the
more likely outside ourselves, nor to suspect them where we are
not at home. It is rather to bring all will towards God under the
steady claims of a common humanity and into the obedience of
an intention which we ask him to search and save. These are
together the motives that can surely belong with the prayers of
praise and penitence and petition which follow, and can move and
mature with them. 'Let God be God' is the call that commands
us both. We will be sharing words, not to blur nor yet to stress
distinction, but to build community—community not less real
but more in that it is honestly circumscribed. Neither can bring
all that we are: but with all that we are we may come.

In coming, we may well find our purposes deepened by the
meditations of those who count themselves strangers to us both.
The selections here have drawn freely from such sources, both
contrary and congenial. The pressures of spirit that may bring
Muslim and Christian together require also an open heart for all
who speak out of the depth of the human condition. Theists have
no proper reason to treat atheists impatiently. There is a kind of

doubter whose reservations measure well the necessary dimensions of faith. We shall better pray for all such if, as Ezekiel said,
we are ready to 'sit where they sit'.

There need, then, be no surprise that Brecht and Camus should
be among our authors, as well as Bunyan and Al-Bakrī, Abū-l-
'Alā as well as Al-Jīlānī. Not that any real anthology of radical
doubt could properly be so scant and fragmentary: it was not our
purpose to seek one, but simply to learn from a few, almost at
random, the size of the human crisis as they have known it. This
alerts all intercession to its proper business and saves the pursuit
of prayer from the protective complacencies, if such they be, of
church walls and mosque courts. No worship will ever hallow, or
suffice, the world, if it is not fulfilled within it.

'Let an enquirer ask the muezzin' runs the proverb. For he is a
man of integrity by fact of his office and, from his vantage point in
the minaret, he has long learned the lie of the city streets like the
palm of his hand. Must not the call to prayer, Christian or
Muslim, command the same inclusive perspective of the human
scene and speak out of the same reliable honesty? If so, then we
must heed the artists and poets of our time, in whom we hear the
language of our own anxiety and see the mirror of our generation.
'It had better be good, or it won't be cheer', the passionate
doubter, Thomas Hardy, used to say, about the Gospel's bidding:
'Be of good cheer.' In that sense we may well say: 'It had better
be alert, or it won't be prayer.' If we are alive to God we cannot
be casual about the world.

There is another angle to this matter that further justifies the
inclusion of a few European—French, Russian, and other—
voices of Western malaise or despair. For in Muslim Asia and
Africa, especially in devout circles, there is a very natural inclina-
tion to castigate, and sometimes to scorn, Western irreligion and
secularity. Much of the indictment is fully deserved. It reflects a
bitter sense of grievance and resentment against Western *mores*
and influences, as disrupters and destroyers of Islamic standards
and Muslim securities. But in the understandable passion of these
strictures, it is all too possible for the inner travail and stress of
the Western soul to be misconstrued or unrecognized. Not all is
vacuity that seems so. The West has to be seen, in part at least,

as the first and most vulnerable victim of human pretensions and temptations, which are rapidly becoming universal in their incidence and menace. It experiences in the most concentrated form the strains of technology, which by their very accumulation may be even more devastating elsewhere.

It is urgent for all cultures somehow to sense and measure the Western crisis as the symptom of their own. We need not imply here, or debate, any comparisons about relative capacities face to face with modernity. What matters is the universalizing of the elements that have made it what it is—the loss of the significant self, the frustrations of mastery, the ills in the pride, the paradox in the plenty. This is why we need the doubters, the minds which register and the arts which epitomize our wretchedness and yearning. Theirs is the burnished glass in which we recognize ourselves. Theirs is the clinical scrutiny which disqualifies any light healing of our hurt.

Yet it is often to such slight healing that orthodox commentary is prone, in its reproach of a Christianity that seriously discusses whether 'God has died'. It can easily seem to the outsider to have disqualified itself from the robust business of a sound religion by its restless thinking and its tenuous authority in its own societies. There is need to pause before all such verdicts are assumed. The Christian tensions, within the travail of the Western mind, have a relevance for every faith. We shall not long be 'alive to God' if we register only a proud or fearful denial of the belief that he is dead. We shall fail to be rightly Islamic, if we see in the permissiveness of the Western ethos only an occasion for gratification about the stouter orthodoxy, or the more totalitarian ethic, of Islam. For the issues belong to *how* God is rightly worshipped in the living world. 'His', says the Qur'ān, 'is *Daʿwat al-Ḥaqq*'. 'To him is the call of truth:' 'his is the prayer of right:' 'It is the real call that is his' (Surah 13-14). Therefore, only with the right worship can we answer aright. This, which is, by definition, the meaning of Islam, is at the heart of the current travail of theology and it reaches out into all the realms of human action, in family, education, nation, trade, culture, community, and peace.

To plead it here, in this way, is not to present a Christian apology, nor to invite a false sympathy, nor yet to forestall

legitimate reproach and advantageous controversy. It is, beyond
all these, a plea for the patient care of integrity and for common
prayer as its most fitting, if only intermittent, expression. If, as
we have argued, there is enough identity about the current world
and at least a discernible rendezvous of spirituality, then we may
be of some relevance to each other on both sides of this responsibility, the contemporary and the eternal, the secular and the
sacred.

It follows that we must be ready to find the inter-penetration of
these two in unlikely places. Christianity and Islam, alike, are
committed to their respective foci of the sacred—holy Scriptures,
holy times and holy seasons, holy acts and forms. But they are
comparably committed also to the permeation of all else by the
claim and meaning of these sanctities. Ramaḍān hallows all the
year in recurring emphasis on the discipline of the fast. Prayer
cleanses the heart while cleansing prepares for prayer. The *Qiblah*
faces one towards Mecca because 'the face of God is everywhere'.
Holy Communion consecrates all social community in its representative offering of the elements of sustenance and hospitality.
Sunday is calculated to take all our days into its symbolic meaning.
This sacramental presence of the sacred in the secular, this
sacramental availability of the secular for the sacred, belong in their
different ways with both Muslim and Christian. To pray by help
of the lively humanness of 'secular' poets or playwrights is only to
give the immediate to the ultimate, to bring the actual to the
relevant, the newspaper to the Scripture. We can see this as a
threefold relationship in which none of us are in the wrong
company. For the sceptics give the measure of the world where
theists must come true.

II

In some sense also they furnish the words. It belongs with the
genesis of this anthology to believe that prayer, in whatever camp
of faith, is a calling of increasing puzzlement to contemporary

men. Many are at ease neither in letting it go, nor in letting it stay. They cannot renounce prayer, any more than they can cease to care about the world. But they cannot well sustain it, in any sure confidence about traditional forms and phrases. All such, we might say, are praying to pray—no more, no less; no more, because from time to time the terms, the assurance, the tidiness, of what their systems afford them, have somehow failed to carry their integrity: no less, because their hearts and wills are deeply alive to the essential wistfulness of life.

In so far as this is so, we are bound to seek forms of prayer in which our loyalty can be creative, unembarrassed, and authentic. We look, as it were, for words which mean more perhaps by saying less, which do not everywhere require the sort of assents and accents we can no longer always bring. Much traditional Christian liturgy, for example, has about it a spaciousness of language, a dignity of expression and a stance of mind, that accord ill with our confusion, our brokenness and anger. They are too chaste and stately for our mood: they are, as it were, such composed compositions. The collects of the Anglican Prayer Books are so largely concerned with security, defence, preservation, continuance; '. . . that Thy church may be . . . preserved evermore . . .': in all godly quietness', in a time when no godliness can be quiet or all quietness be godly. Or, when prayers become adventurous they circumscribe themselves with familiar clichés we cannot readily interpret: '. . . that all Israel may be saved and the fullness of the Gentiles may be gathered in'. We are left wondering about Mao's little books and the lotus-fire in Vietnam or Jan Palach in Prague. Or, when they strike the note of jeopardy and risk, it is in an archaic idiom: '. . . by Thy great mercy defend us from all perils and dangers of this night . . .' when those are probably neither the perils, nor the night of the soul, we really mean.

Likewise with the piety of mosque and *khalwah*, of *namāz* and *ward*.[1] 'O God, write for Thy servants a release from the fire, security from punishment and transit on the straight path and a portion in the garden.' 'Call me hence as a Muslim and let me die

---

[1] *Khalwah*, a place of meditation or devotional community; *Namāz*, a popular term for ritual praying; and *Ward*, or 'rosary', a Ṣūfī form of prayer or 'liturgy'.

a believer.' Again, the same personal preoccupation and :
assured context of ideas. 'O God, send down blessing up(
Muḥammad, and his companions, and his people. . . . O God,
seek refuge with Thee from the accursed devil and from th
distraction and ambush of the grave.' Yet how are we to relat
this refuge to the exposures of the world and the *Allāhu akbar* t
the stalking evils of violence and poverty that are also 'grea'
before our eyes?

This is not to say that the traditions of prayer have becom
invalid or that they do not yet satisfy many of the faithful. It i
to say that their meaning has to find voice also in an idiom whic
does not first estrange men's realism while it invites thei
reverence, which does not bewilder their thoughts in undertakin
to utter them. It is, therefore, the outsider, the agnostic, whor
we need in alerting our language to what it must embrace—n(
in order that we should retreat from faith, but that we ma
retrieve its witness in this day.

From these pressures there is emerging a pattern of prayin
which is, as it were, simply meditative, not so much—as ofte
hitherto—about the mysteries of faith, but rather about th
tumults of the world. It reads the newspaper with a sort
reflective responsibility for its picture of the dailiness of life. .
wants to react in God and for God to what it perceives around it (
the plight and the passion of society. It is perhaps at times n
more than a steady refusal to be casual or callous (words which i
our sort of mass-information-media-world have become almo
synonymous). It knows that there is a corporate guilt abo(
hunger, war, and tragedy, and a corporate menace in ignoranc(
enmity, and violence. Such 'praying' cannot always, or readily, l
fitted into prayers. But even wordless it means a will to l
participant, a desire to atone, a purpose to care, a readiness
understand. It is a negation of indifference and a commitment
compassion, which it does not defer or evade because of reserv
tions, still unresolved, about theology or ritual. Rather it sens
that the care of these is best satisfied in caring about the wor
It wants to be alive to God in being alert to mankind.

'The poor of the world are my body', he said,
'To the end of the world that shall be:
The bread and the blankets you gave to the poor,
You'll find you have given to me', he said,
'You'll find you have given to me.'[1]

r, in the different idiom of the eleventh century poet, Al-
ıjjām:

> Fairer is the manuscript
> When the reed is clipped:
> Clearer runs the message, when
> There's a trimming of the pen.
> Dimly burns the lantern: but
> When its wick is cut
> Perfect will its lustre be,
> Through the wick's deficiency.[2]

From this very restraint of profession, if such it needs to be,
hile still bent towards our fellows, we may well return, in due
me, to those incomparable petitionaries of the old tradition.

. . graft in our hearts the love of thy Name, increase in us true
ligion, nourish us with all goodness and of thy great mercy keep
s in the same . . .
hat it may please Thee to strengthen such as do stand: and to
omfort and help the weak-hearted: and to raise up them that fall:
nd finally to beat down Satan under our feet.

uch is the deliberate principle of inclusion in this anthology and
ie hope from its use.

12

3o we reach the end of the survey and the beginning of the
rney. All belongs within the long Abrahamic, Semitic, mono-
stic tradition of faith, a threefold community with its single

Sydney Carter: Quoted by permission of Galliard Ltd., Gt. Yarmouth.
Quoted from *Moorish Poetry*, trans. by A. J. Arberry, Cambridge,
3, p. 80.

geography of origins and its kindred sense of the patriarchs. A trilateral relationship runs through every bilateral exchange.

Our concern, then, involves no neglect of the Hebraic. With open heart it makes a deliberate effort in respect of a specific field—a field more readily served, circumstantially and otherwise, by its present limitation, where the material anyway is so vast and selection so fragmentary. Islam and Christianity together embrace great populations, distributed almost universally and covering more than two-fifths of humanity. They have a physical, political and social relevance to each other not surpassed by any other pair of faiths. They inter-penetrate, with crucial consequences for peace and nationhood, in many spheres in east, middle, and west Asia, and Africa, north, west, and east, and in the Western hemisphere. It is clear that their mutual duties are rightly distinguishable within the plural and general relationships of each with all.

That interrelation has a peculiarly urgent character in one particular area of contemporary crisis—that of the confrontation of Israeli Zionism and the Arab spirit. Some summary attempt must be made here to take its measure from within the perspectives of the prayers that follow.

By force of history, Arabness is intimately identified in, and identifiable by, Islam. Muḥammad is the Arab Prophet and the Qur'ān is Arabic Scripture. By factors of still longer history Christianity is closely tied with Hebrew antecedents in patriarch, psalmist, prophet, and Messiah. The lineal political expression of that Hebrew history in Zionist form in the territorial State of Israel has collided violently and tragically with the twentieth century soul and life of the Arab, Muslim nations. The bitter impasse is symbolized by the political disappearance of Palestine, the polarization of Arab/Israeli conflict and of Arab/Jewish populations in the Middle East.

It is urgent to realize what this means for Arab Christianity. Its faith-links are with the Hebraic in Isaiah, in the Gospel and in Paul, while its heart-links are with the Arab soul in its case and cause about Israel. It thus incurs, in vexing personal intensity, the whole burden of the present equation between the Hebraic and the Israeli. How ambivalent to sing: 'Blessed be the Lord

God of Israel', in or across from the Israel of Moshe Dayan. How arduous to reckon with an authentic Old Testament when its literal meanings have now such an exultant animus against oneself. 'Moab is my washpot: upon Philistia will I triumph.' The Christian mind labours under this heavy liability of Old Testament elements which Zionism has bound over to Israeli politics and thus to Arab tragedy.

This paradox of 'Israel' as at once adversary and ancestor strains the Christian sense of Old Testament indebtedness to a point where its authority can no longer emotionally obtain. By the decisive logic of statehood, Zionism identifies itself wholly and inevitably with the norms of political and military power, and so throws into radical ambiguity the relationships which properly belong with Biblical faith. Christians—Arabs among them most of all—are politically bereaved of a spiritual history, a history disallowed, not by their defection, but by the decisions of its own trustees.

This situation deserves far more careful thought among outsiders than it normally receives. It bears directly on the relevance of this anthology. The Christian minorities that shoulder it are anyway small minorities indeed, numerically, save in the Lebanon. If one subtracts the non-Arab elements, notably the Armenians, the minority circumstance becomes even more acute. It is also steadily accentuating through a variety of causes belonging with the over-all circumstances affecting the region.

But beyond simple statistics of Near Eastern Christianity is the fact that the Christian communities live under the entail of a nineteenth-century history largely fashioned from without. Fully committed as they are to Arab identity and to its stake in the long tragedy of Palestine, they inherit from those decades a legacy of experience in which, as minorities, they were often delivered, emotionally and physically, into the protective solicitude of Western powers, who used them in their own interests or intrigues within the Ottoman domains. In twentieth-century Arab perspective, it is these same powers which are inevitably seen as the precursors and accomplices of the State of Israel. The Balfour Declaration, the Mandate and then the State, in their corroborative sequence, are taken as the perpetuation, in Zionist form, of that alien, external imperialism which elsewhere in the world is politically withdrawn. Seen in Arab eyes as a Western intrusion in the Arab world on this model, Israel as a State is involved in an impasse of hostility, tragic for its own ideals and yearnings and bitter in its cost in refugees, in suffering and in humiliation.

Whatever the ultimate Arab decisions they cannot relate to these dimensions in 'sectarian' form. To speak, isolatedly, from the Christian side, would only be to sound like the old nineteenth-century 'tool' of the 'Western' interest. Even to seem to discount tragedy is not to begin to heal it. There can be no unilateral reaction to Israel from within Arab Christianity—Coptic, Orthodox, Latin, or any other. All are bound within the common crisis of Arabness where alone the ultimate burden can be understood and borne. It is seen by Arab Muslim and Arab Christian alike as standing in the terms imposed by the Zionist decision for the state. How readily defensible those terms are every observer knows who ponders the European tribulations of Jewry and feels with the age-long love of Zion. These things only make more agonizing the sorrows implicit in their climax. For the Arab world is innocent of the guiltiness of Europe and has its own sense of love and justice over the territories where Zion stands. What, then, is the Zionism fitting to Zion? Good is evil here and evil good with a complexity that makes anguish for every lively imagination and fuel for every burning resolve.

When the sixth-century B.C. Israeli was in captivity by the ever flowing waters of Tigris and Euphrates, he looked for a deliverance by which his captivity would run dry and peter out, 'like the rivers in the south', those flash streams of the Negev where no permanent irrigation could then be imagined. The Arab Palestinian looks for a like correction of his history. But the rivers that inundate him flow permanently on. They are well sustained from beyond and they have nowhere else to flow.

> I tell you naught for your comfort
> Naught for your desire,
> Save that the sky grows darker yet
> And the sea rises higher.

Prayer would seem a fragile, futile, foolish thing to set amon such forebodings and such forces, were it not the way, surer than both comfort and desire, into the purpose and the sovereignty of God. As Charles de Foucauld discovered, it is capable of interposing a strange hiatus into every bitter exchange and of stilling the confusion while God is named. As a cry for the Divine Lordship it belongs with all the faiths and present history cannot overwhelm it. Wherever prayer begins it concerns one humanity and reaches towards the final questions—not, now, states, or territory, or frontiers, or rights, but rather: 'What sort of humanity are we all becoming?' 'What are we doing to each other and, therefore, to ourselves?' Prayer, being the perspective of the Divine presence, has to do with the limits of power and the transformation of pain. 'It is not well', as Stephen Crane wrote in *The Red Badge of Courage*, 'to drive men into final corners.' What should the rule of God mean? 'When fire is high', said Sa'dī, 'it burns the world; extinguish it today while it may be quenched.'[1] These are the urgencies of Godward petition, however remote they may seem from predictable developments. Prayer also helps to restore the perspective of the world and of history and to recover the great precedents of anguish and of peace which forbid us to fear or to crave that somehow ours is the only tragedy. And it serves also, for those in neighbouring immunity or spectator wisdom, to deepen their sympathies and lengthen their thoughts.

'I can hardly tell why it should be', wrote the English Kinglake in his travel classic of the desert, *Eothen*, 'but there is a longing for the East very commonly felt by proud-hearted people when goaded by sorrow.'[2] What, then, can proud-hearted people *in* the east do, 'goaded by sorrow'? They cannot *go* to their remedy. They have to pray in the chaos of Jerusalem: they discover that there is no more bitter irony in all holy writ than the saying: 'They shall prosper that love thee' (Psalm 122:6). For this is the city of attrition and crucifixion. It is not well that it should be visited only in the tourist-ticket-travel of today, so different from the rigours and sharing of realities required of the pilgrims of the past. All such reflections, and many more, bring us again, surely, where we started in conceiving this anthology to be at once feasible and

---

[1] *Gulistan*, op. cit., p. 238.
[2] London, 1844, Chapter 8, p. 84.

E

imperative. This—and not any hope of other fields of conclusion about so deep a tragedy—was their only purpose.

13

A few miscellaneous points remain. Quotations from the Qur'ān are more numerous than from the New Testament. This is primarily because the Qur'ān, in its unique way, is both document and recital. It is devoutly memorized by all devout Muslims and such learning forms the basis of all theological education. Being thus known by heart, it pervades the thinking and the phrasing of the Muslim soul. Even its sequences from verse to verse affect the run, and perhaps the logic, of association in the Islamic way of things. Without exact parallel outside Islam, this characteristic is fostered by the non-chronological arrangement of the Qur'ān, which, so to speak, gives the verses a definitive quality as they stand and roots them, in their own right, in the heart. It follows that Quranic recitation is a form of prayer. Ṣalāt takes the Fātiḥah in this way and the example runs through all. In its observations and warnings and examples the Qur'ān focuses the themes and terms of Islamic devotion. What, in the end, is prayer, if not such focus of the imagination and the will?

Conversely, a quantitative measure might indicate that Christian sources of actual prayer composition are somewhat more frequent. The reason, again, takes us to the habits of articulation or of invocation we have already noted. The reflective prayers that depend upon the extracts from the Scriptures of either faith or from the moderns of neither are, unless otherwise indicated, the work of the compiler, as are the renderings of the Qur'ān. It will be clear to any expert reader that the prayers employ images and words which both can recognize as their own.

The collection on its Muslim side makes no conscious distinction between Sunnī and Shī'ah, since what is, or was, at issue between them does not enter into its concern. Nor does the heritage of Ṣūfī Islam, of the great mystics and orders of piety, have any dominant share. This is not an anthology of Sufism. Were it so, it would not be true to the breadth of Islam. While it can be claimed that Sufism, from time to time, has proved the mainstay of Islamic religion in the flux of the world, the dullness of orthodox theology or the carelessness of states, it would be wrong to allow it to monopolize the stage. The Ṣūfī poets, indeed, are here: but they are in no sense alone. Western sympathies have been sometimes tempted to isolate the Ṣūfīs unduly from the full stream of Muslim spirituality. This is not only unfair to history. It is lacking in perception about the demands of modern relationship, where in some senses mysticism is the least apt of all in bringing men 'alive to God'.

The index of sources will suffice as proof of the range of our enlistment. Close to twenty original languages and almost thirty countries, from the Java Sea to the Caribbean, are represented and many of the wellnigh fourteen Muslim and the twenty Christian centuries.

The index of themes is meant to facilitate the use of the prayers by individuals or by those responsible, in schools or groups, and on occasions, for corporate worship. The pages themselves, however, are free of headings other than the main grouping of praise, penitence, and petition, so that the sense of each page can make its own point, as the reader may recognize and take it. The threefold division itself in no way isolates its elements.

There are always minds that turn enquiringly to practical matters. Are we to pray unshod, as Muslims must and as many Christians, for example in India, already do? Or will footwear remain as a kind of symbol of Christian identity? Are men to have their heads covered, which many Christians prohibit but Muslims readily allow? Are ablutions necessary before any kind of praying? These are all points of some relevance. The fact that formal liturgies are not involved dispels some of them, or eases their solution. They all fall, surely, within the mutual courtesies we have to pre-suppose. There is hardly need here to particularize about how local and personal sensitivity will agree to deal with these—and doubtless a host of other—matters. Where the way forward belongs with individual use they do not even arise at all.

In all the foregoing many questions have been left to silence.

Conventional controversies have gone unnoticed. Other minds would no doubt have seen other points clamouring for review and perhaps placing emphatic veto on the whole. Others too would have brought together a quite different set of choices to illustrate their case, whether pro or con. What we have is no more than a gesture of hope and an attempt to show its grounds.

All readers, convinced or sceptical, will be well aware that there are forces and factors within our faiths, interpreting their duties and understanding their loyalties in ways divergent from these. But we need not despair. In a recent book of essays, Eldridge Cleaver, of the Black Panther Party in the U.S.A., describes his uneasy turn back from total, negative hatred to a struggling sense of common humanness, still precariously jeopardized by white arrogance, but real and precious. He ascribes his change of soul to the revolt of white youth against their 'establishment' and to the death of Malcolm X who, after pilgrimage to Mecca, repudiated the hate-philosophy of the Black Muslims in the discovery of Islam's one humanity. Cleaver writes:

I have, so to speak, washed my hands in the blood of the martyr, Malcolm X, whose retreat from the precipice of madness created new room for others to turn about in, and I am caught up in that tiny space, attempting a manoeuvre of my own. Having renounced the teachings of Elijah Muhammad, I find that a rebirth does not follow automatically of its own accord, that a void is left in one's vision, and this void seeks constantly to obliterate itself by pulling one back on one's former outlook.[1]

'Room to turn in', however 'tiny', is the crux of the struggle and prayer is its only lodgement in the soul, its only tenure in the hating and the hoping world.

In his fascinating book, *The Lonely African*, Colin Turnbull comments on the familiar pitfalls in the art of translation and cites, in example, a literal, African language rendering of the words of the Gospel according to John (1:1): 'In the beginning was the Word, and the Word was with God and the Word was God.' It ran: 'In the beginning there was a great argument, and

---

[1] In *Soul on Ice*, London, 1969, p. 66.

the argument came with God, and the argument entered into God.'[1]

There has, in truth, almost from the beginning, been long and loaded argument between Islam and Christianity. And the argument, controversially, entered into God, into conflict about his will, his nature, his justice, his knowledge, and his mercy. All of which are very urgent matters. But is there not another way before us of 'entering into God'?

[1] Colin M. Turnbull: *The Lonely African*, New York, 1962, p. 157.

The Song of the Reed

Hearken to this reed forlorn,
Breathing ever since 'twas torn
From its rushy bed a strain
Of impassioned love and pain.

The secret of my song, though near,
None can see and none can hear.
O for a friend to know the sign
And mingle all his soul with mine!

'Tis the flame of love that fired me:
'Tis the wine of love inspired me.
Wouldst thou learn how lovers bleed?
Hearken, hearken to the reed.

JALĀL AL-DĪN RŪMĪ:
The opening lines of his *Mathnawi*

PRAISE

Intention is a central condition of all the acts of canonical duty in
Islamic life.

> O Lord God,
>   inspire, determine and enable
>   the intention of my life,
>   that it be to thine honour.
>
> Seal it as the desire of my heart,
>   the purpose of my mind,
>   the goal of my whole strength
>   that it continue single, clear,
>   immutable, importunate.
>
> O Lord, be this intention, THOU:
>   thy truth, thy work, thy love, thy glory.
>
> Let it govern my words,
>   dwell in my thoughts,
>   purify my dealings,
>   occupy and redeem my time.
>
> Let it bring Thee into all my ways
>   and the ways of those with whom I have to do,
>   Thyself, thy light, thy salvation,
>   thy wisdom, thy worship, thy blessing,
>   Today and always.
>
>   ERIC MILNER WHITE:
>   *My God, my Glory*

Someone said: 'Remember us in your intention. Intention is the
root of the matter. If there be no words, let there be no words:
words are the branch.'

                                   JALĀL AL-DĪN RŪMĪ:
                                       Discourses

To God belongs the praise, Lord of the heavens and Lord of the earth, the Lord of all being. His is the dominion in the heavens and in the earth: he is the Almighty, the All-wise.

Surah of the Kneeling, v. 35

O the depth of the riches both of the wisdom and knowledge of God! How unsearchable are his judgments and his ways past finding out! For who hath known the mind of the Lord? Or who hath been his counsellor? Or who hath first given to him, and it shall be recompensed unto him again? For of him and through him and unto him are all things: to whom be glory for ever. Amen.

The Epistle to the Romans, Chapter 11:33–6

'Tis no matter to amaze
If thy gifts outstripped my praise,
Or thy bounty overfilled
This my vessel, ere it spilled.

ABŪ-L-SALT:
Bounty

Great and marvellous are thy works, Lord God Almighty; just and true are thy ways, thou King of saints. Who shall not fear thee, O Lord, and glorify thy Name? For thou only art holy: for all nations shall come and worship before thee; for thy judgments are made manifest.

The Book of Revelation: Chapter 15:3–4

He is God. There is no god but He. He is the King, the holy One, the Peace, the Trustworthy, the Preserver, the Almighty, the Ever-powerful, the Exalted.

Glory be to God beyond all that idolaters conceive.
He is God,
   Creator,
     Maker,
       Fashioner.
His are the most excellent Names.
All that is in the heavens and in the earth magnifies him, the Almighty, the Wise.

Surah of the Exile, v. 23–4

Great art thou, O Lord, and greatly to be praised. Great is thy power and thy wisdom is infinite. And thee would man praise, man but a particle of thy creation, man that bears about him his mortality, the witness of his sin, that thou resistest the proud.
Yet would man praise thee, he but a particle of thy creation.
Thou awakenest us to delight in thy praise. For thou madest us for thyself and our heart is restless until it rest in thee.
Grant me, Lord, to know and understand which is first—to call on thee or to praise thee? and again, to know thee or to call on thee? For who can call on thee, not knowing thee? For he that knoweth thee not may call on thee as other than thou art.
Or is it better that we call on thee that we may know thee?

AUGUSTINE:
the opening lines of his Confessions

Now unto the King eternal, immortal, invisible, the only wise God, be honour and glory for ever and ever, Amen.

The First Epistle to Timothy, Chapter 1:17

What can I say to you, my God? Shall I collect together all the words that praise your holy Name? Shall I give you all the names of this world, you, the Unnameable? Shall I call you 'God of my life, meaning of my existence, hallowing of my acts, my journey's end, bitterness of my bitter hours, home of my loneliness, you my most treasured happiness'? Shall I say: Creator, Sustainer, Pardoner, Near One, Distant One, Incomprehensible One, God both of flowers and stars, God of the gentle wind and of terrible battles, Wisdom, Power, Loyalty and Truthfulness, Eternity and Infinity, you the All-merciful, you the Just One, you Love itself?

KARL RAHNER:
Prayers for Meditation

It is God who made the earth for you as an abode and the heaven for a building. He fashioned you: comely did he fashion you and with good things did he provide you.
Blessed then be God your Lord, this God, Lord of all being. He is the living God: there is none save he.
Call upon him in sincerity of worship.
Praise be to God, the Lord of all being.

Surah of The Believers, v. 66–7

O infinite God, Centre of my soul, convert me powerfully unto Thee.

THOMAS TRAHERNE:
Thanksgivings for the Body

None more powerful is than he,
And yet how gracious is my Lord.
Of all 'mighties' known to men
He is the mightiest of them all
How gracious is my Lord.

On none depends for any need,
To none in debt is he indeed,
He shaped the world in nothingness,
He is the Creator of one and all.
How gracious is my Lord.

Whatever is, he is the Maker,
Of earth and sky he is the builder:
Nothing concealed from him remains,
He sees and knoweth all that is
How gracious is my Lord.

He is One with no compeer,
His oneness reflects his greatness.
He that hath his friendship
No other friend need seek.
How gracious is my Lord.

He is beginning and He the end,
He is changeless and eternal,
Rahman, gracious is my Lord.

RAḤMĀN BĀBĀ
A Pushtu Poem

He is the First and the Last.

Surah of Iron, v.

His mercy is on them that fear him, throughout all generations.
He hath put down the mighty from their seat, and exalted them
of low degree.
He hath filled the hungry with good things; and as for the rich
he sends them away empty.

The Gospel according to Luke: Chapter 1:50, 52, 53

Praise be to God, sovereign Lord, Author of the universe, who
raises the winds and orders the morning, worshipped in religion
and the Lord of the worlds. Praise be to God for his forbearance,
when he knows all. Praise be to God for his pardon, though he is
all-powerful. Praise be to God for his long-suffering in displeasure, though he is well able to do what he chooses.

Praise be to God, Lord of creation, Source of all livelihood, who
orders the morning, Lord of majesty and honour, of grace and
beneficence, He who is so far that he may not be seen and so near
that he witnesses the secret things. Blessed be he and for ever
exalted.

Praise be to God: he has no competitor to equal him and no peer
to compare with him, and no helper to aid him. With his might
he subdues the mighty and by his greatness the great are humbled.
Whatever he wills by his power he attains.

Praise be to God who hearkens to me when I call upon him, covers
my unworthiness when I have been rebellious and magnifies his
grace upon me. I will not more trangress. I will sing to his praise
and make mention of him in thanksgiving.

Ramaḍān Prayers

To thee be most high praise!
In worshipping thee we have not attained the fulness
of worship,

O worshipped One.

To thee be most high praise!
In invoking thy Name we have not attained the fulness
of invocation,

O thou who art invoked.

To thee be most high praise!
In thanking thee we have not attained unto the fulness
of thanksgiving,

O Thou who art thanked.

To thee be most high praise!
In seeking thee we have not attained unto the fulness
of seeking,

O thou who art the goal.

To thee be most high praise!
In describing thee we have not attained unto the fulness
of description,

O thou who art described.

MUṢṬAFĀ AL-BAKRĪ
Seal of the Five Prayer

Those who attend permanently at the temple of his glory confess
the imperfection of their worship and say: 'We have not wor
shipped thee according to the requirement of thy worship:' and
those who describe the splendour of his beauty are rapt in
amazement saying: 'We have not known thee as thou oughtest to
to be known.'

SAʿDĪ
The Gulistān

We have set in the heavens constellations making them glorious
to behold . . . and the earth We have stretched out, whereon are
borne the great mountains and where We have caused everything
to grow accordingly, providing there a livelihood for you and for
those for whom you take no liability. There is nothing whose
treasure sources are not Ours, and all are constituted from above
in their appointed measure. We send the fertilizing winds and
bring down the rain from heaven, giving you to drink of reservoirs
that are not yours.

Surah of Al-Ḥijr, v. 16, 19–22

O all ye works of the Lord, bless ye the Lord,
    Praise him and magnify him for ever.

O ye mountains and hills, bless ye the Lord,
    Praise him and magnify him for ever.

O all ye green things upon the earth, bless ye the Lord,
    Praise him and magnify him for ever.

O ye children of men, bless ye the Lord,
    Praise him and magnify him for ever.

O ye servants of the Lord, bless ye the Lord,
    Praise him and magnify him for ever.

O ye spirits and souls of the righteous, bless ye the Lord,
    Praise him and magnify him for ever.

O ye holy and humble men of heart, bless ye the Lord,
    Praise him and magnify him for ever.

Benedicite Omnia Opera

F

To God belong the east and the west and wheresoever you turn there is the Face of God. Truly God is All-pervading, All-knowing.

Surah of The Cow, v. 115

Lo! God is here, let us adore
  And own how dreadful is this place:
Let all within us feel his power
  And silent bow before his face:
Who know his power, his grace who prove,
  Serve him with fear, with reverence love.

Lo! God is here, him day and night
  The united choirs of angels sing:
To him, enthroned above all height,
  Heaven's hosts their noblest praises bring.
To him may all our thoughts arise,
  In never ceasing sacrifice.

GERHARDT TERSTEEGEN,
translated by John Wesley

I have only one desire
To feel you close beside me,
As did Moses on the peak of Sinai.

AMĪR HAMZAH:
One Alone

In the Name of God upon my heart
  That its thirst may be quenched.

In the Name of God upon my knees
  That they may be strengthened.

In the Name of God upon the earth,
  That it may be traversed.

ʿABD AL-QĀDIR AL-JĪLĀNĪ:
Wells of Prayer

I asked the earth and it answered me: 'I am not it' and all things whatsoever in it made the same confession. I asked the sea and the deeps and the creeping things and they answered me: 'We are not thy God; seek beyond us . . .' I asked the heavens, the sun and moon and stars, 'nor', say they, 'are we the God thou seekest'.

AUGUSTINE:
The Confessions

Accordingly, We showed Abraham the kingdom of the heavens and of the earth, that he might be one of sure faith. As night darkened round him he beheld a star and said: 'This is my Lord.' But when it set, he said: 'I cannot love what sets.' And when he saw the moon rising he said: 'This is my Lord.' But when it set he said: 'If my Lord does not guide me aright, I shall surely be among the erring.'
And when he saw the sun rising he said: 'This is my Lord; this is greater.' But when it also set he said: 'O my people, I have finished with all your idolatrous things. As for me, my face is towards the One who created the heavens and the earth, as a man of pure faith. I am not a worshipper of false deities.'

Surah of The Cattle, v. 75–9

Glory be to thee, O Lord, glory be to thee.
   Creator of the visible light,
      the sun's ray, the flame of fire.
Creator also of the light invisible and intellectual,
   that which is known to God,
      writings of the law, oracles of the prophets,
      melody of psalms, instruction of proverbs,
      experience of histories,
      a light that never sets.
God is the Lord, who has showed us light.

LANCELOT ANDREWES:
Preces Privatae

You set up the sky like a canopy and spread it out like a tent. By a mere act of will you gave the earth stability when there was nothing to uphold it. You established the firmament . . . and set in order the chorus of the stars to praise your magnificence.

Prayer at the Eucharist:
Apostolic Constitutions

Which was the harder task in creating, you or the heaven he reared? He raised the canopy of heaven and set it in poise. He made the night a cover over it and he brought forth its high noon. And then he laid the expanse of the earth, bringing forth waters and pastures therein, and he made fast the hills to be a joy to you and to your flocks.

Surah of The Spoilers, v. 27–31

O God, I call upon thee by thy great truth, by the truth of the light of thy gracious countenance, the truth of thy mighty throne, by that greatness and majesty, beauty and splendour, power and authority, of thine that uphold thy throne, and by the reality of thy Names, hidden and concealed, which none of thy creatures has pondered.

O God, I call upon thee by the Name that thou has set upon the night that it became dark, and upon the day that it became light, upon the heavens that they spread forth, and upon the earth that it came to rest, upon the mountains that they stood, and upon the seas and valleys that they flow, upon the fountains that they rise and the clouds that they give rain.

Prayers of the Naqshabandi Order

Praise be to him who alone is to be praised. Praise him for his grace and favour. Praise him for his power and goodness. Praise him whose knowledge encompasses all things.

O God, grant me light in my heart and light in my tomb, light in my hearing and light in my seeing, light in my flesh, light in my blood and light in my bones.

Light before me, light behind me, light to right of me, light to left of me, light above me, light beneath me.

O God, increase my light and give me the greatest light of all. Of thy mercy grant me light, O thou most merciful.

ABŪ ḤAMĪD AL-GHAZĀLĪ:
The Beginning of Guidance

Open thou mine eyes and I shall see:
Incline my heart and I shall desire:
Order my steps and I shall walk
In the ways of thy commandments.

O Lord God, be thou to me a God
And beside thee let there be none else,
No other, nought else with Thee.

Vouchsafe to me to worship thee and serve thee
According to thy commandments,
    In truth of spirit,
        In reverence of body,
           In blessing of lips,
               In private and in public,
To overcome evil with good.

LANCELOT ANDREWES:
Preces Privatae

Everything with him has its measure, Knower of the unseen and of the seen, All-great and All-exalted: it is all the same with him whether your word is furtive or open loud, whether you go stealthily in the night or fare forth in the open day.

Surah of Thunder, v. 9–10

O God, All-powerful, true and incomparable, present in all things, yet limited by none, uncircumscribed by place, unaged by time, unhurried by the years, not beguiled by words, not subject to birth, never in need of protection, far above corruption, admitting of no change, by nature immutable, living in light that none can approach, essentially invisible, yet known to all rational beings that ponder on thee lovingly and grasped by those who seek thee because thou art dear to them . . .

Deal with us after thy lovingkindness . . . Bless these people whose heads are bowed before thee . . . make them holy, watch over them, protect them and support them, deliver them from the adversary and all other enemies, guard them in their going out and their coming in.

To thee be all praise, glory, greatness, adoration and worship . . . for ever, age upon age.

Final Blessing in the Eucharist:
Apostolic Constitutions

Vouchsafe to me
A scroll, I pray
My shield to be
In fate's affray.

Let your right hand
Inscribe thereon:
'Praise God most High,
Praise him alone.'

ḤAFṢA OF GRANADA:
The Shield

My God, I love thee thyself above all else and thee I desire as my last end. Always and in all things, with my whole strength and heart and with unceasing labour, I seek thee. If thou give not thyself to me thou givest nothing. If I find thee not I find nothing. Grant to me, therefore, most loving God, that I may ever love thee for thyself above all things in this life present, so that at last I may find thee and keep thee for ever in the world to come.

THOMAS BRADWARDINE:
Archbishop of Canterbury

O God, who art rich and praiseworthy, who createst and restorest to life, who art merciful and loving, make me to abound in what is lawful in thy sight, in obedience to thee and by grace from thee, so that I turn from what is unlawful, from disobedience and from all other than thou.

ABŪ ḤAMĪD AL-GHAZĀLĪ:
The Beginning of Guidance

On you we call, Lord God,
All-wise, All-surveying, All-holy,
The only true Sovereign.

You created the universe:
You watch over all that exists.
Those who lie in darkness,
Overshadowed by death,
You guide into the right road, the safe road.
Your will is that all men should be saved
And come to the knowledge of the truth.

With one voice we offer you
Praise and thanksgiving.

Egyptian Christian papyrus:
Patrologia Latina

By the manifestation of thy surpassing glory, bring me out of every kind of ignorant neglect, wherein I might lose thee at any breath of mine or moment of time. Show to me thy nature as light, lifting off the shadows of mortal being that I may be among the companions of the Face.

To thee, O my God, is the rising and the setting sun: at every turn there is the Face of God.

AḤMAD IBN IDRĪS: *Prayers*

Addressing all well-meaning but unmortified men, wandering aimlessly on the paths of self-love and finding no consolation either in God or creatures, because their hearts are thrown about from one confusion to another, I invite them to turn their backs on the stifling vanities of self-absorption. *Sursum corda:* lift up your hearts.

HENRY SUSO: *The Exemplar*

How excellent is thy lovingkindness, O God.

We commend to thee, Lord, our impulses
  and our incentives,
Our intentions and our ventures,
Our going out and our coming in,
Our sitting down and our rising up.

How truly, meet, and right, and comely, and due,
  In all and for all,
  In all places, times and manners,
  In every season, every spot,
  Everywhere, always, altogether,
To remember thee, to worship thee,
To confess to thee, to praise thee,
To bless thee, to give thanks to thee,
  Maker, Nourisher, Guardian, Governor,
  Healer, Benefactor, Protector of all.

LANCELOT ANDREWES:
Preces Privatae

Praise be to God who feeds us and gives us to drink, who suffices for us and shelters us. How many there are who have none to be to them either sufficiency or haven. In thy Name, O God, I live and in thy Name I die.

O Lord God, I ask of thee, from thy Presence, a mercy by which thou wilt guide my heart and order my concern, a mercy by which thou wilt repair my distractedness and bring back my alertness, a mercy cleansing my works and inspiring my ways, a mercy ennobling what I mean to others and reuniting me with those to whom I belong, a mercy whereby thou preservest me from every evil.

This, O God, is my prayer. Thine it is to hear. This is my yearning. On thee is all my reliance.

> Prayer of the Prophet Muḥammad according to Abū Ḥamīd
> al-Ghazālī

> By the sun and the midday glory
> And the moon that follows after.
> By the day telling its splendour
> And the night that envelopes it.
> By the heaven and its rearing,
> By the earth and its shaping,
> By the soul and its ensouling.

> Surah of The Sun, v. 1–7

All that is in the heavens and in the earth magnifies God: for he is Almighty and All-wise. To him belong the kingdoms of the heavens and of the earth, and unto God is the returning of all things. He makes the night to give way to the day, and the day to the night, and he knows the innermost hearts.

> Surah of Iron, v. 1, 5 and 6

Awake my glory, my lute and harp myself shall wake.
Soon as the stately, night-exploding bird,
In lively lay, sings welcome to the dawn.
List ye! how nature with ten thousand tongues,
Begins the glad thanksgiving.
All hail! ye tenants of the forest and the field,
My fellow subjects of the eternal King,
   I gladly join your matins and with you
   Confess his Presence and report his praise.
O thou, who or the lambkin or the dove,
When offered by the lowly, meek and poor,
Preferest to pride's hetacomb,
Accept this mean essay,
Nor from thy treasure-house of glory immense
The orphan's mite exclude.

O could I search the bosom of the sea,
Down the great deeps descending, there thy works
Would also speak thy residence: and there
Would I, thy servant, like the still profound,
Astonished into silence, muse thy praise.
Vain were the attempt, and impious, to trace
Through all his works the Artificer Divine,
And though no shining sun, nor twinkling star
Bedecked the crimson curtain of the sky,
Yet man, at home within himself, might find

The Deity immense, and in that frame,
So fearfully, so wonderfully, made
   See and adore his providence and power. . . .
The knee which thou hast shaped shall bend to thee,
The tongue which thou hast tuned shall chant thy praise,
And thine own image, the immortal soul,
Shall consecrate herself to thee for ever.

CHRISTOPHER SMART: *Awake my Glory*

'Lift up your hearts!'

Whenever I say the words: *Sursum corda!* my heart and soul seem to be melting away with Divine love and compassion. . . . Reflections set my heart on fire and spread out their hungry flames to ignite the heart of all animate creatures. Sometimes they occur to me singly, sometimes all together. First, I contemplate in spirit all my being, my soul, my body and all my powers, and place all the creatures with which God has peopled the earth, the heavens and the elements.

Next, I consider creatures individually: the birds of the air, the beasts of the forest, the fish in the waters, the plants of the earth, the sands of the seashore, the tiny cobwebs in each ray of sunshine, the snowflakes, raindrops and dewy diamonds, and reflect that each of these creatures obeys God, thus contributing to the mysterious concord of sweet sounds which ascends to the Creator as an unceasing *Te Deum* in praise of his mercy. Then I imagine myself as choirmaster directing this mystical chorus, and I invite and prompt all the members to uplift their hearts and souls to God: *Sursum corda!*

HENRY SUSO:
The Exemplar

It is he who made the sun a splendour and the moon a light, ordaining its phases that you might register the years and make reckoning. He created them with truth alone, distinguishing the signs to men of understanding. Surely in the alternation of day and night and through all God's creation in the heavens and in the earth are signs for those who fear him.

Surah of Jonah, vv. 5–6

I consider my own heart and those of all men and reflect on the joy, love and peace of those who consecrate all their faculties to God's service and the contrasting misery, bitterness, and unrest with which the world repays her devotees. Then I invite all men living on earth to join me in the zealous service of God, saying: 'O poor, imprisoned human hearts, lift yourself above the walls which enclose you! Wake up, sleeping hearts, throw aside the apathy of your sluggish, careless habits. Take flight heavenwards on the wings of a true and complete conversion to the God of all love. Lift up your hearts!'

HENRY SUSO:
The Exemplar

Thy Name be glorified for evermore for all the art which thou hast hidden in this little piece of red clay.
For the workmanship of thy hand, who didst form man of the dust of the ground, and breathe into his nostrils the breath of life. Thy works speaking to me the same thing that was said unto Adam in the beginning: 'We are all thine.'

Even for our earthly bodies thou hast created all things: the influences of heaven,
    Clouds, vapours, winds, dew, rain, hail, snow,
      Light and darkness, night and day,
    The seasons of the year, springs, rivers, fountains,
      Corn, wine and oil, the sun, moon and stars,
    Cities, nations, kingdoms,
      And the bodies of men, the greatest treasures of all,
    For each other.

THOMAS TRAHERNE:
Thanksgivings for the Body

O thou on whose generosity and the beauty of thy customs all petitioners depend, praise be to thee.

ʿABD AL-QĀDIR AL-JĪLĀNĪ:
Wells of Prayer

Have they not beheld the heaven above them? How we established and adorned it in its unbroken reach? And the earth also we stretched out and set thereon the mighty hills, where we made every kind of joyous thing to grow, for insight and for token to every penitent servant. And from heaven we have sent down the blessed rain whereby we make the gardens grow, and grain of harvest and tall palm trees laden with clustered dates, in provision for men, thereby bringing again to life a land that was dead—similitude of 'the coming forth'.

Surah Qāf, vv. 6–11

Be present, merciful Lord, with us thy creatures that our joy in thy creation may kindle into true thanksgiving and season all our dealings in house and market, in producing and consuming. Let the sense of thy bounty hallow our thoughts and our exchanges, for the doing of thy will and the glory of thy Name. Amen.

Love came a guest
Within my breast,
My soul was spread,
Love banqueted.

IBN ḤAZM:
The Ring of the Dove

Do you not see that God it is whom all things praise in the heavens and in the earth and the birds too on wings of flight? Each truly knows its prayer and its praising and God knows their every deed. For to God belongs the kingdom of the heavens and of the earth and unto him is their becoming.

Surah of Light, v. 41–2

Thy beauty shines O God, through all created things
In all this wide, immeasurable universe,
Thou art expressed, revealed,
Brought close and intimate and near.

Thy love, most mighty and most sweet,
In song of birds, in sunset clouds,
In flower, in wind and star,
Is eloquent and tangible and close.

Ungainly, foolish words!
How can mere words,
The mask and darkening of reality,
Express thy Being?
How can mere words
Set forth thy praise?

JOHN S. HOYLAND:
The Fourfold Sacrament

I hold the splendid daylight in my hands . . .
Daylight like a fine fan spread from my hands,
Daylight like scarlet poinsettias,
Daylight like yellow cassia flowers,
Daylight like clean water,
Daylight like green cacti,
Daylight like sea sparkling with white horses,
Daylight like tropic hills,
Daylight like a sacrament in my hands.

GEORGE CAMPBELL:
Litany

My God and my Lord, eyes are at rest, stars are setting, hushed
are the movements of birds in their nests, of monsters in the deep.
And thou art the just who knowest no change, the equity that
swerveth not, the everlasting that passeth not away.
The doors are locked, watched by their bodyguards.
But thy door is open to him who calls on thee.
My Lord, each lover is now alone with his beloved.
Thou for me art the beloved One.

ʿABD AL-ʿAZĪZ AL-DĪRĪNĪ:
Purity of Heart

. . . to see
   Mortals subdued in all the shapes of sleep.

Here lay two sister twins in infancy:
   There, a lone youth who in his dreams did weep:
Within, two lovers linked innocently
   In their loose locks, which over both did creep
Like ivy from one stem: and there lay calm
Old age with snow-bright hair and folded palm.

But other troubled forms of sleep she saw,
   Not to be mirrored in a holy song,
Distortions full of supernatural awe
   And pale imaginings of visioned wrong,
And all the code of custom's lawless law,
   Written upon the brows of old and young.

PERCY B. SHELLEY:
The Witch of Atlas

Lighten our darkness, we beseech thee, O Lord, and by thy great
mercy defend us from all perils and dangers of this night.

The Book of Common Prayer

To him belongs whatsoever inhabits the day and the night.

Surah of Cattle, v. 13

About him all the sanctities of heaven
Stood thick as stars and from his sight receiv'd
Beatitude past utterance.

JOHN MILTON:
Paradise Lost

The duteous day now closeth,
Each flower and tree reposeth,
Shade creeps o'er wild and wood.
   Let us, as night is falling,
    On God, our Maker calling,
Give thanks to him the Giver good.

Now all the heavenly splendour
Breaks forth in starlight tender
From myriad worlds unknown.
   And man the marvel seeing,
    Forgets his selfish being,
For joy of beauty not his own.

Awhile his mortal blindness
May miss God's lovingkindness
And grope in faithless strife.
   But when life's day is over
    Shall death's fair night discover
The fields of everlasting life.

PAULUS GERHARDT:
Hymn at Nightfall

All things suppliant unto thee are beloved of thee. O God, I call
upon thee by thy majesty at its most radiant, for every splendour
of thine is truly splendid.

Ramaḍān Prayers

Let man ponder over the food he eats: how we poured down
rains abundantly and opened up the earth, making grain to grow
therein and grapes and green fodder and olive trees and date palms
and thickly bearing orchards, fruits and pastures, providing for
you and for your flocks.

Surah: 'He Frowned', v. 24–32

Lord God, out of your kindness to men, bless the fruits you have
given us and bless your servants gathered for the work of harvest.
Grant salvation also to those who possess these fruits that, having
the abundance that comes from you, they may show to the poor
the kindness that is also yours. To that end accept our whole
worship.

Patrologia Orientalis

O Lord God, whose compassions fail not, grant us grace so to
recognize and receive thy mercies that we may fashion our own
selves after the same pattern of kindliness and care, for the praise
of thy great Name.   Amen.

Bless, O Lord, we pray thee, our taking of bread and let it be, in
our dependence, for gratefulness; of our community, for sign;
and in our using, for comfort and strength; and thine be the
praise this day and always.   Amen.

O Lord, who has taught us to acknowledge in daily bread a debt
to our fellows, known and unknown, grant us in the strength
thereof to live in truly human bonds of compassion, for thy truth
and thy love's sake.   Amen.

G

O thou whose beauty no thoughts can encompass.

O thou whose perfection no vision can conceive.

Invocations from *Ḥirz al-Jawsh*

Spring leaves upon the emerald plain
Embroideries of green again . . .
Again the daffodils have spun
Their dances with the wind and sun.
Anemones the rivals are
Of roses that bedeck the car
Of state, the roses hang their head
And glow more sorrowfully red:
Whereas the lily doth unite
Within herself all heaven's light.

ABŪ-L-ʿALĀ AL-MAʿARĪ:
Poems

What would Heaven and Earth be worth, were there no spectator,
no enjoyer? As much, therefore, as the end is better than the
means, the thought of the world whereby it is enjoyed is better
than the world . . . The world within you is an offering returned,
which is infinitely more acceptable to God Almighty, since it
came from him that it might return unto him.
Wherein the mystery is great. For God hath made you able . . . to
give and offer up the world unto him, which is very delightful in
flowing from him, but much more in returning to him. . . . Let
all your actions proceed from a sense of this greatness, let all your
affections extend to this infinite wideness . . . and let all your
praises arise and ascend from this fountain.

THOMAS TRAHERNE:
Centuries of Meditations

I say, too, that the admiration we feel at works of craftsmanship is akin to the wonder we feel at the works of nature. For what craftsmanship produces is from one point of view a work of nature, inasmuch as it is effectuated by dint of natural forces. Thus the engineer is worthy of our praise who succeeds in moving a heavy weight: but would he not have much greater claim on our admiration if he could make a model capable of handling any weight at all! 'It is God who has created both you and all you do.' Blessed, then, be he whose dominion extends through both the worlds of the visible and the invisible and within your own selves also. Do you not comprehend? The light of his majesty shines forth and no veil can overcome it. He knows that which eludes the eye and what is hidden in the heart. For all that exists is by his power alone and is in motion or at rest according to his will. The fulfilment of his will is all their joy and drawing near to his holy presence is their great delight. By their multiplicity they witness to his unity and by their very changes they confess his abidingness. There is nothing that does not celebrate his praise.

ʿABD AL-LAṬĪF AL-BAGHDĀDĪ:
The Book of Instruction

And so to God, Eternal Lord, Master of creation, Maker and Ruler of men,

> Be the glory and the praise,
>
>> from the wonder of our senses,
>> from the skill of our hands,
>> from the powers in our ordering,
>> from the purpose of our being,
>> from the offering of our worship,
>
> To him be the dominion in all things everywhere.
>
> Amen.

PENITENCE

O thou who acceptest penitent acts.

Thou who art greatly beneficent.

Thou who hearkenest unto those who call.

Thou who knowest hidden things.

O thou before whose greatness everything is humbled.

O thou before whom everything bows in awe.

O thou by whose command the heavens and the earth abide.

O thou in whose fear all things obey.

Thou goal of all hopes: thou refuge of every outcast.

O Master of the covenant and promise.

O thou who bestowest our requests.

O thou who discoverest the distress of every weary soul.

O thou who concealest every blemished thing.

O thou companion of every lonely soul.

O thou who befriendest me in my solitariness.

O thou who companionest me in my loneliness.

O thou who art faithful in covenant.

O thou who bestowest our desires.

O Lord of majesty and power.

Invocations from *Ḥirz al-Jawsh*

The mind of man, as it must be stirred up in the morning, so must it also in the evening, as by a note of recall. It is called back to itself and to its Leader by a scrutiny of self, by prayers and thanksgivings.

There are many hiding places and recesses in the mind. The heart is deceitful above all things. The old man is bound up in a thousand folds. Therefore, take heed to thyself . . . We think him not safe who is undefended by the arms and guard of prayer.

LANCELOT ANDREWES:
Preces Privatae

O our Lord, take us not to task, if we forget or miss the mark. O our Lord, lay not on us a burden like that which thou didst lay on those before us. O our Lord, lay not on us that which we have no strength to carry. Pardon and forgive us. Thou art our Master.

Surah of The Cow, v. 286

Have mercy upon us.
Have mercy upon our efforts, that we
Before thee, in love and in faith,
Righteousness and humility,
May follow thee, with self-denial,
Steadfastness and courage,
And meet thee in the silence.

Give us a pure heart that we may see thee,
A humble heart that we may hear thee,
A heart of love that we may serve thee,
A heart of faith that we may live thee.

DAG HAMMARSKJÖLD:
Markings

He knows the treachery of the eyes and what the breasts conceal.

Surah of The Believers, v. 19

I looked at myself as I then was. Worldly interests encompassed me on every side . . . When I considered the intention of my teaching, I perceived that instead of doing it for God's sake alone I had no active motive but the desire for glory and reputation. I realized that I stood on the edge of a precipice.

ABŪ ḤAMĪD AL-GHAZĀLĪ:
The Deliverer from Wandering

With 'No Admittance' printed on my heart,
I go abroad and play my public part and
Win applause. I have no cause to be
Ashamed of that strange self that others see.

But how can I reveal, to you, and you,
My real self's hidden and unlovely hue?
How can I un-deceive, how end despair
Of this intolerable make-believe?

You must see with God's eyes, or I must wear
My furtive failures stark upon my sleeve.

BASIL DOWLING:
Signs and Wonders

Almighty God, unto whom all hearts are open, all desires known, and from whom no secrets are hid: cleanse the thoughts of our hearts by the inspiration of thy Holy Spirit, that we may perfectly love thee and worthily magnify thy holy Name.

The Book of Common Prayer

Lord, thou knowest that I am a hundred hundred times worse than thou has declared. But beyond my exertion and action, beyond good and evil, faith and infidelity, beyond living righteously or behaving disobediently, I had great hope of thy lovingkindness. I turn again to that pure grace. I am not regarding my own works. Thou gavest me my being as a robe of honour: I have always relied on that munificence.

JALĀL AL-DĪN RŪMĪ: *Mathnawi*,
'The Man who looked back on the Way to Hell'

O God, I am ashamed to lift up my face to thee.
   For I have done evil in thy sight,
   Not keeping thy commandments,
   Not doing thy will,
And now my heart kneels to thee,
   Beseeching thy goodness.

I have sinned, O Lord, I have sinned,
   And know my iniquities.
   I pray thee, remit to me, remit to me,
Nor reserve evil for me, nor condemn me.

For thou art God, the God of penitents.
   Show in me all thy lovingkindness,
   And save me, though unworthy,
For thy great mercy.

Let thy tender mercies speedily prevent us,
   For we are brought very low.
   Deliver us and purge away our sins,
For thy Name's sake.

LANCELOT ANDREWES:
Preces Privatae

O my God, how gentle art thou with him who has transgressed against thee: how near thou art to him who seeks thee, how tender to him who petitions thee, how kindly to him who hopes in thee.

Who is he who asked of thee and thou didst deny him, or who sought refuge in thee and thou didst betray him, or drew near to thee and thou didst hold him aloof, or fled unto thee and thou didst repulse him?

Thine, O Lord, is the creation and the authority.

By what is hidden of thy Names and by what the veils conceal of thy splendour, forgive this restless soul, this anguished heart.

O God, we seek in thee refuge from all abasement save unto thee: from all fear save thine: from all poverty save with thee.

O God, as thou hast kept our faces from prostration to any save thee, so keep our hands from being stretched out in petition to any save thee. For there is no god but thee.

Verily I was among the wrongdoers. But praise be to God, the Lord of the worlds.

Prayers of the Naqshabandi Order

Praise be to God. O God, thou art the One to whom we give thanks. I pray the Lord to forgive us for those things which we have done and those things which we shall do in the future. Lord God, drive away from us all sorrow and the envy of enemies, and deliver us from the evil of this world and the next.

ABUBAKAR TAFAWA BALEWA:
Shaihu Umar

O God, thou hast many claims on me for what is between me and thee, and there are many claims against me in my relation to the world of thy creation.

O God, release me of that owed to thee and bear for me that which is between me and thy creation.   *Pilgrimage Prayers*

God in heaven,
Let me really feel my nothingness,
Not in order to despair over it,
But in order to feel the more powerfully
The greatness of thy goodness.

SØREN KIERKEGAARD

O Lord God, thou knowest my secret and my open things. Receive my plea. Thou knowest my need. Grant, therefore, my petition. Thou knowest all that is in my soul.

O Lord God, I ask of thee a faith to occupy my heart and a true assurance, whereby I may know that nought shall ever befall me outside thy purposed will for me. Let me be well pleased with whatever thou allottest me, O thou Lord of majesty and honour.

Prayer of Adam, according to Abū Ḥamīd al-Ghazālī:
The Reviving of Religion

Almighty . . .   By thy mercy
Forgive   Abase me,
My doubt,   By thy strictness
My anger,   Raise me up.
My pride.

DAG HAMMARSKJÖLD: *Markings*

Be clothed with humility: for God resisteth the proud and giveth grace to the humble. Humble yourselves, then, under the mighty hand of God, that in due time he may exalt you, casting all your care upon him: for he cares for you.

The First Epistle of Peter: Chapter 5:5–7

O God, preserve me from evil allurements and keep me from all tribulations. Make good both my inward and my outward man and cleanse my heart from hatred and envy. Let not any man have any issue against me.

O God, I seek of thee to lay hold of the good and to forsake the evil, as thou knowest them. Undertake, I pray thee, for my protection and give me simplicity in my living and by clear guidance a way out of all dubiety and victory with the right in every argument.

Grant me to be just, both in anger and in good pleasure and submissive to what the decree brings. Make me moderate both in poverty and wealth, humble in word and deed and truthful in jest and earnest.

O God, I have trespassed in my relationship with thee, and I have trespassed in my relationship to thy creation. O God, forgive my trespasses against thee and bear off from me my trespasses against thy creation. Enrich me with thy goodness. For thou art plenteous in forgiveness.

O God, enlighten my heart with knowledge and employ my body in thy obedience. Save me from the machinations of my heart and occupy my thoughts with thy esteem.

Prayers of the Naqshabandi Order

Make me, O Lord, to give myself unto mine own penitence and to thy praises, to withdraw into penitence and blessings.

Open my mouth to bless thy holy Name: thou shalt open my lips and my mouth shall show thy praise. But for me, O Lord, sinning and not repenting, and so utterly unworthy, it were more becoming to lie prostrate before thee, and with weeping and groaning to ask pardon for my sins, than with polluted mouth to praise thee.

Howbeit, trusting in thy huge goodness, I give praise. Accept the praises I desire to sing, I an unworthy sinner, indeed unworthy. But would God I were devout and grateful unto thee.

To thee I give thanks: thee I worship, I praise, I bless, and thee I glorify.

Thou art worthy, O Lord, to receive praise and thanks, whom I, a sinner, am not worthy to call upon.

Thee I call upon, thee I worship, with the whole affection of my heart, I bless now and evermore.

LANCELOT ANDREWES:
Preces Privatae

O Lord God, ever forgiving, I pray thy pardon here and hereafter, pardon in my relationships and my possessions.

Lord, hide my shortcomings and preserve my spirit within me. Take away my obstacles and keep me on the right hand and on the left, from behind and from beneath, in every undertaking.

With thee be my refuge from all that lurks below me.

ABŪ ḤAMĪD AL-GHAZĀLĪ:
The Reviving of Religion

O you who believe, avoid idle supposition. Suspicion is an evil thing. Do not spy on one another and backbite. Would any of you like to eat his brother like carrion? loathsome thought! Hold God in awe.

Surah of The Apartments, v. 12

Beware of suspicion, the falsest of falsehoods.

Tradition noted by Ibn Ḥazm

> A newspaper is a collection of half injustices
> Which . . .
> Spreads its curious opinion
> To a million merciful and sneering men . . .
> A newspaper is a court
> Wherein everyone is kindly and unfairly tried
> By a squalor of honest men,
> A newspaper is a game
> Where his error scores the player victory,
> While another's skill wins death.
> A newspaper is a symbol;
> It is feckless life's chronicle,
> A collection of loud tales
> Concentrating eternal stupidities.

STEPHEN CRANE:
War is Kind

Forgive, O Lord, our sanguine carelessness, our reading-up of gossip and innuendo, our reading-in of malice and ill-will, our casual appetite for easy defamation, our heedlessness of human tragedy in the daily 'press' of passing information.

Make us to read between the lines the misery and destiny of fellow men and their call to our compassion in judging and in caring. We pray so for thy truth's sake.   Amen.

Isaiah calleth princes thieves. What! Princes thieves? Did they stand by the highway side? Did they rob or break open any man's house or door? No! no! That is a gross kind of thieving. *Omnes diligunt munera:* 'they all love bribes'. Bribing is a princely kind of thieving.

HUGH LATIMER:
Sermons

No graven images may be
Worshipped, except the currency.

Thou shalt not steal — an empty feat
When it's so lucrative to cheat.

Bear not false witness: let the lie
Have time on its own wings to fly.

Thou shalt not covet: but tradition
Approves all forms of competition.

ARTHUR HUGH CLOUGH:
The Latest Decalogue

Lord, thy command unto the good is clear. But there is a perversity in our hearts and deviousness in our bosoms. We bring an outward service to thy law, reserving the while our own cunning and advantage. We give to the commandment the tribute of pretence and use the law itself to evade its righteousness.

We circumvent thy statutes by becoming anonymous. We deplore evil and allow the big collective to pursue it. We build and blame the economic order for our alibi and hide our ungodliness in remote consent, exonerated by a customary tolerance. Evil is too abstract for our imagination, too subtle for our double-mindedness.

O God of truth, turn us to the truth, turn us to thyself. Amen.

The enormous tragedy of the dream in the peasant's bent
shoulders.

EZRA POUND:
First Pisan Canto

> Will you be astonished
> If these flowing fields
> No longer grow crops for a privileged class,
> Refuse to add to the blood sucker's fat . . .
> And that burden-hunched peasant
> Stands fearless, upright as an unstringed bow,
> And lifts on that back a quiverful of arrows?
> Will you not be afraid?

MUFAKRUL-ISLĀM:
Bengali Poems

O Lord God, who has granted to men in our time an ever larger
empire over the material world, have mercy upon our affluence
and upon our poverty, upon our pride and upon our shame.

Grant to our generation to learn the hallowing of science by the
poetry of worship that we may be saved from the menace in our
own competence.

Is the climax of our technology to be the dark valley of our despair? Centuries of toil have reached for the wealth we now attain.

Is it to be the easy plenty of the few amid the harsh privation of
the many, a world of scientific neighbourhood across a chasm of
inequality? Shall the promise of leisure be only a more wearisome
curse and the long dream a proven illusion?

Let the humanity that masters nature become the servant of thy
praise, whose alone and always are the power and the dominion
and the glory.   Amen.

I was an hungred and you gave me no meat: I was thirsty and you gave me no drink: I was a stranger and you took me not in: Sick and in prison and you visited me not.

Then shall they answer him, saying: 'Lord, when saw we thee an hungred, or athirst, or a stranger, or naked, or sick, or in prison, and did not minister unto thee?'

Then shall he answer them saying: 'Verily I say unto you, inasmuch as you did it not to one of the least of these you did it not to me.'

The Gospel according to Matthew, Chapter 25:42–5

God rebuked Moses, saying: 'I am God, I fell sick; thou camest not.'

Moses said: 'O transcendent One, thou art clear of defect, what mystery is this? Explain, O Lord.'

God said unto him again: 'Wherefore didst thou not kindly ask after me when I was sick?'

He answered: 'O Lord, thou never ailest. My understanding is lost: unfold the meaning of these words.'

God said: 'Yea, a favourite and chosen slave of mine fell sick. I am he. Consider well: his infirmity is my infirmity, his sickness is my sickness.'

JALĀL AL-DĪN RŪMĪ:
Mathnawī

Make us, Lord,
to see and serve thy glory,
in seeing
and salving
the pain of the world.

H

O my God, thou art my confidence: of thee I seek protection lest there be in me any source of thy unpleasing. O my God, save me from all inadequacies and let all my doings be to thy good pleasure. O thou Lord of glory and honour, grant me the crown of knowledge, knowledge of thy unity and thy Divine nature, so that I may be occupied with thee alone.

Make real to me, O God, the glory, the beauty, the excellence, the majesty, the perfection that are thine, the light and the splendour. Let me know the sweetness thereof in my own soul that I may be precluded from self-preoccupation.

Let the vision of thee keep me from the thought of myself and let me thus depart never from the keeping of thy Divine laws granted by revelation.

AḤMAD IBN-IDRĪS:
Prayers

Let us pray for our common good to our God, the Beneficent. May God give us grace on the left and on the right, with blessings of respect, and let his will be done.

O Lord, protect us: let our hearts be in command. Where we go give us opportunity on the right hand and on the left. Let us be obedient. Cover us.

O God, give us patience, that our lives may be dignified. Separate us from troubles that abound on earth. Give us a good compass to guide us home.

AḤMAD BASHAIKH IBN ḤUSAIN:
Swahili Poem

Forgive, O Lord, what we have been
Direct what we are,
And order what we shall be,
For thy mercy's sake.   Amen.

I take refuge with the Lord of the daybreak.

Surah of The Daybreak, v. 1

> From this fog-bound earth of ours
> We take refuge in thee.
> O rest of our souls,
> Escaping like birds from a broken cage
> To the keen, clear air, and the sunny uplands
> Where thou dwellest, and with thee
> Find release from meanness of spirit,
> From jealousy, slander, hypocrisy,
> From selfish ambition,
> From the insidious darkness that broods
> And breeds in our wills and hides
> The vision of good and the pathway of peace.
> We take refuge in thee:
> Let us walk honestly in the daylight.

JOHN S. HOYLAND:
The Fourfold Sacrament

O God, with thee I take refuge from doubt and idolatry and discord and hypocrisy and evil, from wrong seeing and from the perversion that is worship of worldly things, wealth, family and offspring.

Pilgrimage Prayers

Lord, thou hast created me and I am thy servant. On thy covenant and promise is my utmost reliance. With thee be my refuge from the evil I have done, pleading before thee thy mercy upon me and upon my ill-doing. Forgive me, then, for there is none that forgivest transgression, only thou, O Lord God.

ABŪ ḤAMĪD AL-GHAZĀLĪ:
The Reviving of Religion

Dawn, attack, booty, violence, shame, death.

By the snorting war-horses that strike fire with their hoofs as they storm forward at dawn, a single host in the midst of their dust-cloud.

Man is indeed ungrateful to his Lord; witness what he does. Violent is he in his passion for wealth. Is he not aware that their Lord is cognisant of everything about them on that day when the tombs yield up their dead and all men's hidden thoughts are public knowledge?

Surah of The War-Steeds, v. 1-10

The story, Lord, is as old as man,
Man the raider, the plunderer, the conqueror,
Defiling the light of dawn with the conspiracies
Of night,
Perverting to evil the fine instruments of nature,
Dealing fear among the tents and the homesteads
Of the unsuspecting and the weak,
Confiscating, purloining, devastating.

The passions are more subtle in our time—
The fire-power of bombs for the dust-clouds of cavalry,
Napalm and incendiary and machines in the skies,
Yet dealing the same curse of destruction,
In the same defiance of the sanctity of humankind,
The same gracelessness against the majesty on high.

By the truth of the eternal exposure,
By the reckoning of the eternal justice,
By compassion upon kin and kind,
By the awe of thy sovereignty,
Turn our deeds, O good Lord, repair our ravages,
Forgive our perversities.
O God, give peace, give grateful peace.   Amen.

O God, watch over me always, in my work, in my words, in the thoughts of my heart. O God, have mercy on me, in this world and in the world to come.

O God, have mercy on me, for I have sinned against you, mortal that I am. But kind and gentle Master, forgive me.

O God, hide not your Face from me when I come before you. Do not turn away from me when you pronounce your sentence on our lives—the lives we have lived in the open and the lives that have been ours in secret.

O God, do not let me give way to disloyalty. May the enemy find nothing in me that he can call his own. O God, sharpen my will: may it be like a sword and cut out all sinful thoughts from my heart.

O God, as you calm the sea with a word, so drive out the evil passions from my sinful nature.

SHENUTE:
Coptic Prayers of Dair al-Abyad, Egypt

I beg of you, my Beloved,
Pour down the dew of your mercy,
Extinguish the blackening flame,
That my faith in you may live anew.

AMĪR HAMZAH:
In Darkness

My help in poverty, my refuge in distress.

My restorer in faintheartedness, my healer in distraction.

O thou who makest an end of evil deeds.

O thou in whom every complaint comes to an end.

Invocations from *Ḥirz al-Jawsh*

O God, thou art God, King, manifest Truth, from of old exalted in power and might, the only abiding, the ever-living and eternal, the Almighty and supreme Disposer, the All-victorious, other than whom there is no god.

Thou art my Lord and I am thy servant. I have done evil and wronged my own soul. I have acknowledged my transgression, so pardon thou all my wrong-doings, O thou forgiving One, gracious, merciful, patient and compassionate.

O my God, I praise thee, for thou art ever praised and praise-worthy. I thank thee, who art ever thanked and worthy of thanksgiving, for all the gifts of desire thou hast granted even unto me, for the blessings of accomplishment thou hast brought to me, for all that of thy goodness thou hast bestowed upon me. By thy kindness embracing me thou hast brought me in where thy truth belongs and thou hast caused me to know it.

Thanks be to thee for all thy gracious benefits and for thy steadfast favour toward me in protecting me from calamity and answering my petitions when I call upon thee in supplication and entreaty. When I cry unto thee in sincere and humble yearning and cast myself in hope upon thee, I find thee all I need. I take refuge with thee where'er I be.

Be an ever present neighbour to me, gracious, righteous and beneficent, watching over all things, giving victory over every adversary and forgiving all wrong-doings and transgressions and covering with a veil all unworthinesses.

AḤMAD AL-TĪJĀNĪ:
Prayers

Double they are in their hearts, cloaking themselves to hide from him. He knows well their secret selves and what they disclose. He perceives their very hearts.

Surah of Hūd, v. 5

Inasmuch as one couldn't condemn others without immediately judging oneself . . . one had to practise the role of a penitent to be able to end up as a judge . . . I stand before all humanity recapitulating my shame without losing sight of the effect I am producing . . . We are odd, wretched creatures and if we look back over our lives there is no lack of occasions to amaze and scandalize ourselves.

ALBERT CAMUS:
The Fall

God of truth, is there about our very penitence that which needs to be repented of?

a satisfaction in the very sense of guilt, whereby we can now condemn those we consider hardened and complacent?

a crooked recovery of our pride, in the very postures of humility, a secret arrogance in being lowly?

a fraudulent self-reproach the better to console ourselves, or to impress the world, or get a cheap immunity from action?
Make thy pardon a very fire to purge.

O think me worth thine anger, punish me,
Burn off my rusts and my deformity,
Restore thine image so much, by thy grace,
That thou mayest know me, and I'll turn my face.

JOHN DONNE:
Sacred Poems

PETITION

O thou whose mercy embraces all.

O thou whose signs are clear proof for the observant.

O thou to whom the path is open for those who intend
   to find it.

O thou who in thine exaltedness art near.

O thou whose Face alone abides when all else perishes.

O thou whose signs are in the horizon.

O thou unto whose company is all desire.

O thou who art the desire of the ascetic.

O thou in whom, obeying, the obedient find salvation.

O thou in thanks to whom is the triumph of the faithful.

O thou security of the fearful.

O thou whose word is always apposite.

O thou who art ever aware of what thy servants need.

O thou whose hands are stretched out in mercy.

O thou to whom all pride is hateful.

O ever wealthy, never impoverished,

O All-sufficient, never sustained.

Invocations: from *Ḥirz al-Jawsh*

Come forward and seat yourself with ink and paper. I have matters at heart that I have longed to tell you. Now that you are near, write: 'In the Name of God.'

When you have thus acknowledged the Name of God the mighty, then let us pray for his bounty, as God shall deem fit for us. A son of Adam is nought and the world is not ours, nor is there any man that shall endure for ever. . . .

This prayer of faith, if one prays, is ever granted. I am thy poor handmaiden, one burdened with many troubles: I pray thee, lighten them, O Lord, do thou unburden me. I pray to thee in haste as to matters that I cannot judge. Do thou bring me unto happiness; mayest thou deliver me from evil.

O Lord, fulfil for me matters that I cannot accomplish, nor can I even think of one of them, that they shall come to pass.

Lord, do thou cause me to rejoice. Bring the good near to me. Remove the evil from me so that I do not meet with it.

Utendi wa Mwana Kupona, Swahili poem

O Lord God, make me whole, in body, in hearing and in seeing. There is no god save thou. I beseech thee, Lord, let it be well with me beyond the judgment. I ask thee life beyond the grave and the blessed vision of thy gracious Face, yearning to behold thee, all hurtful ill apart, all devious evil spent. I seek refuge with thee from wronging and from being wronged, from enmity within me and against me, and lest I come by any sin or guilt thou pardonest not.

ABŪ ḤAMĪD AL-GHAZĀLĪ:
The Reviving of Religion

Should any among you see evil activities, he should change them with his hand. If he cannot do that he should change them with his tongue. And if he cannot do that he should change them with his heart.

> Tradition of the Prophet, noted by Muslim and by Ibn Khaldūn

With our hands, Lord,

> with the touch that cares, with the skill that tends, with the healing that restores, with the energies that serve and seek the good.

This world, Lord, change it with our hands.

With our tongues, Lord,

> that otherwise so lightly scorn or grossly damn it. Give us the words of sanity and peace, of compassion and goodwill, the few words that draw the sting of anger, the honest words that take the part of truth, the warm words that melt the enmity and reach the isolation of our fellows.

This world, Lord, change it through our tongues.

With our hearts, Lord,

> change it with our hearts. Change it *in* our hearts and through them by our bearing of its pains, our yearning for its righteousness, our striving for its unity, our ministry to the binding of its wounds.

For always in the hearts of men its crisis turns.

Save it, Lord, in our hearts.   Amen.

Petition

I sit and look out upon all the sorrows of the world,
    and upon all oppression and shame:
I see the wife misused by her husband,
I see the treacherous seducer of young women,
I mark the ranklings of jealousy and unrequited love
    attempted to be hid.
I see these sights on the earth.
I see the workings of battle, pestilence, tyranny,
I see martyrs and prisoners,
I observe the slights and degradations cast
    by arrogant persons upon labourers, the poor,
    and upon Negroes and the like:

All these—all the meanness and agony without end—
I sitting, look out upon,
See, hear and am silent.

WALT WHITMAN:
I Sit and Look Out

Let me, rather bow, Lord, and look in,
Know my own heart, party to these wrongs,
By action or by apathy, by consent,
By guilty innocence, by connivance, by neglect,
By the very silence
When I merely sit and observe.

Kindle my heart, Lord, let me kneel and look up,
Bear in my spirit these plagues in men's deeds,
Give to the anger, the shame and the yearning,
The voice of petition,
Love men aloud in thy Presence,
Carry the vast anonymous
In the aspiration of mercy, in the arms of compassion,
Set the energy of prayer against the wiles of the devil,
Share with the travail of love in the ways of mankind,
See, hear, and cry,
Forgiveness from God.   Amen.

That it may please thee to bless and keep all thy people.

That it may please thee to give to all nations unity, peace and concord.

That it may please thee to give us an heart to love and fear thee and diligently to live after thy commandments.

That it may please thee to succour, help and comfort all that are in danger, necessity and tribulation.

That it may please thee to strengthen such as do stand; and to comfort and help the weak-hearted; and to raise up them that fall; and finally to beat down Satan under our feet.

That it may please thee to preserve all that travel, by land or by water or by air, all women labouring of child, all sick persons and young children and to show thy pity upon all prisoners and captives.

That it may please thee to defend and provide for the fatherless children and widows and all that are desolate and oppressed.

That it may please thee to have mercy upon all men.

That it may please thee to forgive our enemies, persecutors and slanderers and to turn their hearts.

That it may please thee to give and preserve to our use the kindly fruits of the earth, so as in due time we may enjoy them.

We beseech thee to hear us, good Lord.

THOMAS CRANMER
The English Litany

Peace be upon you and the mercy of God.

'Tis long that peace has fled from earth;
Yet the mind unexhausted quests for peace.
We've walked in crowds many: like evening birds,
Have searched for peace in shadows and in light;
We've searched for peace in the green of the fields,
In the sound of nocturnal waves and urban roads,
And in the heaven's thick shades.
'Tis long that peace
Has fled from our earth.

SHAMSUR RAḤMĀN:
Poems of East Bengal

The sword is a sheathed rivulet, to whose brink
Death comes to drink:
The lance a bow that drips a crimson flood
And fruits in blood.

IBN ʿABDUS:
Sword and Lance, Cordoban verse

O God, thou art peace. From thee is peace and unto thee is peace.
Let us live, our Lord, in peace and receive us in thy paradise, the
abode of peace. Thine is the majesty and the praise. We hear and
we obey. Grant us thy forgiveness, Lord and unto thee be our
becoming.

Prayer at the close of *Ṣalāt*

And so I go to God to make my peace,
Where black nor white can follow to betray.
My pent-up heart to him I will release
And surely he will show the perfect way
Of life. For he will lead me and no man
Can violate or circumvent his plan.

CLAUDE MCKAY:
The Pagan Isms

See, in yonder field,
The tall cornstalks yield
Before the summer wind,
Bringing to mind
Squadrons streaming out
Of battle in sheer rout,
And the poppies red,
Where the wounded bled.

'IYĀD IBN MŪSĀ:
Corn in the Wind, Moorish Poetry

Mutual counsel is the right pattern for them.

Surah of Counsel, v. 38

We beseech thee, O Lord our God, to set the peace of heaven within the hearts of men, that it may bind the nations also in a covenant which shall not be broken, to the honour of thy holy Name.

Cleanse us with the cleanness of thy truth and guide our steps in inward holiness.

Give concord and peace to us and to all living on the earth, as thou gavest to our fathers, when they prayed to thee, believing truly and ready to obey the All-powerful, the All-holy.

Grant to those who rule and lead us on earth to use aright the sovereignty thou hast bestowed upon them. Lord, make their counsels conform to what is good and pleasing unto thee, that, using with reverence and peace and gentleness the power thou hast granted them, they may find favour in thy sight. Thou only hast the means to do this, this and more than this. Glory be thine, now in the present age and age after age.

CLEMENT OF ROME:
Epistle to the Corinthians

Let the peace of God rule in your hearts, to which also you are called in one body; and be thankful.

The Epistle to the Colossians, Chapter 3:15

Song of kinsmen as they water their camels:

> They are all here ready,
> They belong to us.
> How splendid and useful they are!
> And they are standing ready.
>
> I set my foot on the well,
> O Master of the world,
> O God, the Just, make our task easy.
>
> You will be cooled,
> Come forward slowly.
> Put your mouth to it with blessing.
> It is devoid of evil:
> Your shrivelled bones
> Are now moist and full again.
>
> When they are standing ready,
> And the clansmen all are present,
> None must leave till all are watered.

Anonymous, Somaliland: *Camel-watering Chant*

Lord of the world, grant us wonder, give us reverence, subdue us to courtesy, guide us to unity, school us to gratitude.
Let us know our mastery to be of thy mercy. Let thy peace rule, in the great and in the small.

> Give us peace with thee,
> Peace with men, peace with ourselves,
> And free us from all fear.

DAG HAMMARSKJÖLD:
Markings

I

And war is not aught but what you know well
And have tasted oft.
When ye set her on foot,
Ye start with words of little praise,
But the mind of her grows with her growth,
Till she burst into blazing flame.

ZUHAIR:
poet of the Jāhiliyyah: *Muʿallaqah*

Forgiveness had we for Hind's sons:
  We said: 'These men our brothers are:
The days may bring them yet again
  They be the folk that once they were.'

But when the ill stood clear and plain
  And naked wrong was bare to day
And nought was left but bitter hate,
  We paid them in the coin they gave.

We strode, as stalks the lion forth
  At dawn, a lion wrathful eyed:
Blows rained we, dealing shame on shame,
  And humbling pomp and quelling pride . . .

Poem of the Jāhiliyyah: *The Banū Zimman*

Lord, make me an instrument of thy peace. Where there is
hatred, let me bring love: where there is injury, pardon: where
there is doubt, faith: where there is despair, hope: where there is
darkness, light: where there is sadness, joy: and all for thy
mercy's sake.

FRANCIS OF ASSISI

The more he strives to injure me
  The greater is my clemency.
So when the wick is cut, its light
  Shines all the clearer through the night.

IBN AL-ḤAJJ:
Poem

You are straitened in your own selves: . . . be enlarged.

The Second Epistle to the Corinthians, Chapter 6:12–13

Out of Ireland have we come.
Great hatred, little room,
Maimed us at the start.
I carry from my mother's womb
A fanatic heart.

W. B. YEATS:
Collected Poems

Lord, there are many such,
Dwelling in narrow resentments,
Embittered by wrongs that others have inflicted,
Confined to harsh enmities,
Imprisoned in spirit by despair at evil deeds,
Drained of hope and bereft of peace,
Left to great hatred in this world.

Have mercy, good Lord, upon all these
Whose world, through human malice,
Despairs of human kindness.

Judge and turn their oppressors.
Release again, for the fearful,
The springs of trust and goodness.
Give them liberty of heart
The liberty of those who leave room
For the judgment of God.

Enlarge our hearts, O God,
That we may do battle against evil
And bear the sorrows of the weary,
And seek and serve thy will.
Great art thou, O Lord.
There is nought that is a match for thee.   Amen.

O my Lord, enlarge my heart.

Surah of Ṭā Hā, v. 26

Your soul may well be consumed in pain for yearning after the
unbelieving.

Surah of The Cave, v. 6

> Can bread give strength, or feed,
> Unless it first be broken for the need?
> Or shall the vine, with grapes uncrushed,
> For others yield its wine?

JALĀL AL-DĪN RŪMĪ:
Mathnawi

O Lord, whose service requires all that a man has, grant us in our
hearts the grace of self-giving and the power of sacrifice.

Fit us for the costs of truth and the labours of compassion. Make
us able for the calling which is not by power or might but only by
thy Spirit.

Enable us to live in courage beyond the appearances of the present
or the entail of the past. Teach us the strength by which to hold
with any lost cause of thine until it can be truly won.

Grant us the benediction of the peace-makers in the things of
reconciliation that force and state cannot attain. Give us en-
durance, not grim and hard, but gentle and joyous in the peace
of thy eternity. Show us the long-suffering that is more strong
than anger, more ultimate than hate.

As by broken bread the peoples of the world are fed, so make us to
serve their good by a ready consecration of our wills, according to
thy purpose, who art blessed in mercy, now and evermore. Amen.

O my people, how is it with me that I call you to salvation and you call me to the fire?

Surah of The Believers, v. 41

Let us lie in wait for the righteous man, because he is not for our turn, and he is clean contrary to our doings: he upbraideth us with offending the law. . . . The very sight of him is a burden to us, because his manner of life is unlike that of others and his ways are strange. We are esteemed of him as false coin and he abstaineth from our ways as from filthiness . . . Let us test him with insults and torture, that we may find out how gentle he is and make trial of his forbearance . . . But they knew not the mysteries of God.

The Book of the Wisdom, Chapter 2:12–22

We thank thee, O God, for the patience of truth in thy servants the prophets, of whom evil men made trial in perversity and contempt. In their integrity for thy Name, thy law and thy mercy keep righteous faith with the world. Even in the sign of hatred men recognize their prophets. By the evil that they bear wrong stands at once condemned and overcome. In their steadfastness, thy power fulfils its righteous purpose.

For their goodly fellowship, we praise thee, O God. Lord of thy faithful servants, make us to learn both our judgment and our salvation, that in our time we may be doers of thy will and servants of thy glory, to the praise of thy Name.   Amen.

If it is said to them: 'Worship the compassionate Lord', they say: 'What is this—the compassionate Lord?' 'Are we to worship just at your behest?' And they are only the more alienated.

Surah of Salvation, v. 60

I have no other pictures of the world apart from those which express evanescence and callousness, vanity and anger, emptiness, or hideous, useless hate . . . futile and sordid fits of rage, cries suddenly blanketed by silence, shadows swallowed up for ever by the night. What else have I to say?

EUGENE IONESCO:
Notes

Grant to us, O merciful Lord, whom thou hast called to faith in thy compassion

—a mind for the distrust that besets our fellow men at the very sound of such assurance, hurt and broken as they are by the stresses of the world and the oppressiveness of evil:

—a heart to serve them in the goodness of truth, a heart large enough to take the honesty of their scepticism and meet it in the honesty of faith:

—a patience in the commendation of truth resourceful enough, by the gift of thy mercy, to outstay the suspicions of the cynical, the alienations of the angry, the fears of the betrayed, the apathy of the defeated:

a gentleness fashioned after the pattern of thy mercy, O compassionate Lord of men.   Amen.

Did he not find thee an orphan and sheltered thee?
Find thee wandering and led thee?
Find thee needy and suffice thee?

Then do not oppress the orphan,
Nor repel the suppliant.
The grace of your Lord—let that be your theme.

Surah of The Forenoon, v. 6–11

Would that you knew what the steep is!
It is the freeing of the slave,
Or giving food in the hungry day
To an orphan near of kin,
Or to some needy soul in his distress.
Such are believers indeed:
Patience and mercy are their counsel,
Their counsel to each other.

Surah of The Land, v. 11–17

In part we know it, Lord,
The hard road of compassion,
The strenuous demands of mercy,
The steep ascent of heaven.

But the counsels of bitterness and hatred
Come so quickly to our lips,
So plausibly to our reason.
We do well to be angry, contemptuous, outraged,
We, the exploited, the displaced, the cheated,
We, the ill-used.

Yet make our distresses patient, our counsels gentle.
Let us not refuse the rugged climb
Into lovingkindness,
Out of mere level orthodoxy
And a faith of the shadows.
Make us believers indeed, after thy heart.   Amen.

Aspirations half-mast, hopes benumbed,
Desires under pessimism succumbed . . .
Some humiliation always to stab the rejoicing,
Every smile moist with a touch of chagrin.
Faces and features corrupted by artifice,
Laughter poisoned with innate malice . . .
Only the outer clothing, the gorgeous attire,
Hearts weeping for bitterness of life's satire . . .
Neither passion, nor excitement, freshness nor gaiety.
This is all our entire society.

JOSH MALIHABĀDĪ:
Our Society, Urdu Poetry

The night, the street, street-lamp, drugstore,
A meaningless dull light about.
You may live twenty-five years more
All will still be there. No way out.

You die. And all again
Will be repeated as before.
The cold rippling of a canal.
The night, the street, street-lamp, drugstore.

ALEXANDER A. BLOK:
Russian Poems

Our *cry*. . . .
    the things we feel but cannot pray. . . .

Let our cry *come*. . . .
    from our despair it comes, from our fear. . . .

Let our cry come, *Lord*. . . .
    Name we cannot comprehend, power we cannot tell,
    Love we cannot trace. . . .

Let our cry come, Lord, *unto thee*.

Petition

Houses God has permitted to be established where his Name is
commemorated and men . . . celebrate his praises.

Surah of Light, v. 35

The message of these bare and empty walls
I bow to, I revere.
But don't you see? why surely you must know
That for the last time faith is with us here?
She has not crossed the threshold yet to go,
But all is swept and bare.
She has not gone for good and closed the door.
But yet the hour has struck. Kneel down and pray.
For you will pray no more.

FYODOR I. TYUTCHEV: *Russian Poems*

Lord, in our day there are those who seek thee:
There are those who seek thee not.

Yet the *place* of worship may not well distinguish them.
Habits there evade thee, being customary,
And there are those without who seek in absence
And mark their yearning by their protest.

Make us alert who pray that the walls
Of due religion do not insulate our prayers
From the outsider's world,
Nor the outsider from our cares.
Are these homes of prayer only museums of our history?
Symbols of our culture and poems of our architects?
Is the mark of doom on every holy place?

Sceptics also have gone into museums while faith abides.
Yet prayerlessness is a heavy thing
And darkens our time most sorely.
Lord, we continue to pray: let it not be as mere
Survivors of the secular, but truly revivers of the sacred. Amen.

Our hearts have built this sanctuary to the glory of your Name before ever hand laid stone upon another. May the temples we build within ourselves be as beautiful as the house built of stone. May your kindliness bring you to dwell in both kinds of temple. For our hearts, no less than these stones, bear the mark of your Name.

God, who is All-powerful, could have made himself a house as easily as he brought the world into existence, with a wave of his hand. But he preferred to build man himself instead and man in turn to build for him. Blessed be the mercy that showed us such love.

He is Infinite and we are finite: he built us the world and we build him a house. What a wonderful thing that men can build a house for the God of all power, who is present everywhere, whom nothing escapes. He lives among us out of his compassion towards us and he binds us to himself with his love.

To him be all praise and glory and dominion.

BALAI, of Aleppo:
Syriac Hymn for a church hallowing

To purify oneself, to remember the Name of the Lord and to pray—this is well-being.

Surah of The Most High, v. 14–15

We pray Almighty God that he will set us among those whom he has guided and led to the truth, those whom he has inspired to think on him so that they forget him not, those whom he has preserved from the evil of the flesh so that they choose him above all else, those whom he has devoted to himself so that they worship none save him.

ABŪ ḤAMĪD AL-GHAZĀLĪ:
The Deliverer from Wandering

An olive neither of the east nor of the west, whose oil is almost incandescent without the touch of fire: light upon light . . .

Surah of Light, v. 34

Though it is out of the east that the sun rises . . .
It burns and blazes with inward fire
Only when it escapes the shackles of east and west . . .
That it may subject all horizons to its mastery.

MUḤAMMAD IQBĀL
Jāvid Nāmā

I call upon thee, O God, by the Names inscribed around thy throne. I call upon thee by the Names written upon thy Seat. I call upon thee. O God, by the Name written upon the leaves of the olive tree.

I call upon thee, O God, in the mighty Names with which thou hast named thyself, those of them that I have known and those I have not known.

Prayers of the Naqshabandi Order

O Lord God, who hast made us of different nations but one mankind, whose light rises in the east and reaches unto the west yet belongs to the entire heaven and to all the earth, grant us in thy light to see light.

So govern and order our human diversities that they may serve the whole peace of men, that from the rising of the sun to its going down, thy Name may be great among the nations and the nations blessed in the confession of thy Name, who art exalted above all thy works.   Amen.

Say: 'Call upon God or call upon the Merciful: make either invocation, for his are the most excellent Names. Be neither strident nor speechless. Set your heart on the due path of prayer.'

Surah of The Night Journey, v. 110

Our confidence is in thee,
Who art from the beginning of the creation.
Thou hast opened our eyes within us
That we might know thee, who alone art Most High.

Curb the loftiness of the proud,
Frustrate the designs of the evil-seekers,
Lift up the lowly and bring the mighty down.
Give riches and poverty, life and death.

Thou art the God of all flesh.
Into the deeps thou dost gaze,
Vigilant over all that men are doing.
Thou art our help in danger
And savest us from despair
Creator and sustainer of all that is spiritual.

We pray thee, Lord, to help and defend us,
Deliver the oppressed, pity the insignificant,
Raise the fallen, show thyself to the needy,
Heal the sick and bring back the wanderers,
Feed the hungry, lift up the weak,
Take off the prisoners' chains,
Let every nation come to know thou art God.

The earth is thy creation, Lord,
Such competence is thine in creating,
Such goodness is apparent in the world we behold.
Forgive us our sins, our injustice, our warring deeds.

CLEMENT OF ROME:
Epistle to the Corinthians

O Lord, save thy people and bless thine heritage:
Govern them and lift them up for ever.
Day by day we magnify thee,
And we worship thy Name ever, world without end.
Vouchsafe, O Lord, to keep us this day without sin,
O Lord, have mercy upon us, have mercy upon us:
O Lord, let thy mercy lighten upon us,
As our trust is in thee.
O Lord, in thee have I trusted,
Let me never be confounded.

Te Deum Laudamus

Truly in God have I trusted, my Lord and your Lord.

Surah of Hūd, v. 56

O God, I could not do without thy help and thy righteousness, thy goodness, thy strength and thy beneficence, not even for the twinkling of an eye.

I am thy servant, O God, from the time thou didst set me in this vale of soul-making, of thought and experience, that thou mightest observe what I sent forward into the world of immortality and decision, the abode of the blest.

Make me, O God, thy free man.

O God, I have no thought of thee but what is beautiful. I see in thee nought but graciousness. Thy goodness is to me all embracing. Thy works in my sight are perfect. Ever sure is thy mercy and thy righteousness is full of forgiveness. Thy bountifulness toward me is constant and perpetual and unremitting are thy benefits.

AḤMAD AL-TĪJĀNĪ:
Prayers

Death leans to death! nor shall your vigilance
Prevent him from whate'er he would possess.

Dark leans to dark! the passions of a man
Are turned about all transitory things.

The centuries are morsels of the night.

ABŪ-L-ᶜALĀ AL-MAᶜARĪ
Quatrain

Thus command my heart and soul:
  'Let us forward go.'
Thought under iron-heels,
Ideals under house-arrest,
Fill my cup of woe,
  'Let us forward go.'

ᶜABDUL-ḤALĪM JOSH
Sindhi Poem

O Lord God, who hast called thy worshippers to steadfastness in
perplexity and to a good courage in the face of evil, renew in us
in this our day the strength of will and patience of soul whereby
thy servants before us fulfilled their calling in thy will.

Let no discouragement deflect us from the straight path and no
dismay deter us from our avowed intent to follow it. Give us
boldness that we may defy all that—thy grace apart—would
daunt our spirits and beset our way with fears.

Give us a sure confidence in the issue of our lives that no powers
of earth or hell may hold us in the thrall of false anxiety. Rather
let us labour night and day to make good a pilgrim's constancy,
come wind, come weather. By thine aid and goodness, hear our
prayer.

Adapted from JOHN BUNYAN
The Pilgrim Song

I say unto you: 'Love your enemies, bless them that curse you, do good to them that hate you, and pray for them which despite-fully use you, and persecute you, that you may be the children of your Father who is in heaven. For he makes his sun to rise on the evil and on the good and he sends rain on the just and on the unjust.'

The Gospel according to Matthew, Chapter 5:44–5

> Broadcast widely if you can
> The benevolence you plan,
> Troubling not if near or far
> Its receiving stations are.
>
> So the rain has little care
> What it falls upon, or where,
> Irrigating equally
> Barren rock and fertile lea.

SIRĀJ OF ANDALUSIA:
Poems

I ask of God mercy and forgiveness and I pray that he would be pleased to lead us to the fountain of the pure knowledge of himself. For he is gracious and liberal in his kindness.

Peace be to you my brother, whom it is my duty to aid, and the mercy and blessing of God be upon you.

IBN TUFAYL:
Concluding Prayer in: *Alive, Son of Alert*

My brothers, the love of God is a hard love. It demands total self-surrender.

ALBERT CAMUS:
The Plague

Had the truth followed their passions, the heavens and the earth
and all within them would have altogether gone awry. But we
have brought men their Reminder, flout it as they do.

Surah of The Believers, v. 73

> Observe the conduct of these people closely:
> Find it estranging, if not very strange;
> Hard to explain even if it is the custom,
> Hard to explain even if it is the rule.
> Observe the smallest action, seeming simple,
> With distrust. Enquire if a thing be necessary
> Especially if it is common.
> We particularly ask you,
> When a thing continually occurs,
> Not, on that account, to find it natural
> In an age of bloody confusion,
> Ordered disorder, planned caprice,
> And dehumanized humanity, lest all things
> Be held unalterable.

BERTOLT BRECHT:
Plays

Lord, save us from easy acquiescence in the way of things. Let us
not think the deceits around our senses the only mirror of
humanity. Keep our minds that they move in more than headlines
and detect the shape of prejudice or the slant of greed. Alert us
against the cheap purveyors.

Make us open to the judgment that saves because it faithfully
condemns. Let us not resign to sub-humanities. Give us humour
and ardour to deplore and not disdain, to repudiate and yet
transform. Our very restlessness denies us a deceptive rest and
the eternal Reminder abides, the more patient if the more refused,
and to thee is our returning.   Amen.

A man said to the universe:
'Sir! I exist.'
'However', replied the universe,
'That fact has not created in me
A sense of obligation'.

STEPHEN CRANE:
War is Kind

We will show them our signs in the horizons and in themselves,
that it may yet be evident to them that it is the truth. Does it not
suffice thee that thy Lord is witness over all things? Does he not
encompass everything that they should be thus in doubt that it is
with him they have to do?

Surah of The Expounded Signs, vv. 53-4

Doubters, Lord, are many in our day
People daunted by the fear of their irrelevance,
Oppressed by the vast infinity of space,
Redundant in the very progress of technology,
Powerless within the organization of power,
Finding no meaning to their insignificance.

Make us, Lord, to serve their reassurance wisely,
Lest the sense of thy mercy
Seem an empty wistfulness
They will not stay to test,
Suspecting we are shallow men
Or merely doctrinaire.

So dwell in our thoughts and make godly our ways
That men may read thy signs within them
And without and it may suffice them
To know that thou art God, God alone,
Embracing all things, and knowing
Even where thou art not known.   Amen.

K

We have sent down iron with its mighty potential and its diverse utility to men, that God may know those who are for him and his messengers, siding with the hidden mystery.

Surah of Iron, v. 25

Look! Here I stand, among lathes, hammers,
Furnaces and forges, among a hundred comrades.
   There are iron-forged spaces above me,
   Girders and angle bars on the sides,
   Rising seventy feet, bending right and left.
They are tied to the cupola rafters and
Like a giant's shoulders support the whole iron frame.
   They are impetuous, sweeping, strong.
   They require a still greater strength.
I look at them and I stand straighter;
New iron blood pours into my veins,
And I am growing taller, steel shoulders
And immeasurably strong arms grow out from me.
I merge with the building's iron.
Then I stretch myself,
With my shoulders I push out the rafters
   The highest girders and roof . . .
   And I am going to shout one single iron phrase:
The victory will be ours!

ALEKSEI K. GASTEV:
Russian Poems

By thy leave, O Lord, from ore and mine, in furnace and foundry, with lathe and bore, we shape our tools and take our powers. Civilization through metallurgy, culture by electronics, iron and the soul. Grant us, we pray thee, so to wield power as to learn reverence, so to take the force that we may bow to the mystery of nature, so to yield to thy authority that we rightly know our own.

Amen.

That thou makest rightly obey power, her bounds know. Those past, her nature and her name is changed. To be then humble to her is idolatry.

JOHN DONNE:
Third Satire

Man indeed transgresses in thinking himself his own master. For to your Lord shall all things return. . . . Nay! Do not obey him: worship and draw closer (to God).

Surah of The Blood Clot, v. 6, 7, 8 and 19

Truly idolatry is great wrong.

Surah of Luqmān, v. 12

Lord, around us are the manifold works of men,

—states, structures of trade and power, machines and media, principalities of science and race, customs and cultures—all by the dominion entrusted to men's hands under your sovereignty.

With these vast achievements come also usurpations and injustices, tyrannies and prides, working the alienation of the very humanity that boasts them.

Save us, Lord, from every false worship, from all deceiving arrogance. Let us be absolute for thee alone. Keep us from every idolatry of thing, or power, or thought, or means, or claim.

For yours is the Kingdom of the heavens and of the earth and in your rule is our peace. Amen.

Do not live on usury doubling your wealth many times over: have fear of God.

Surah of The House of ʿImrān, v. 129

Those who devour usury shall be as men deranged by the touch of Satan when they stand before God.

Surah of The Cow, v. 275

> With *Usura* hath no man a house of good stone
> Each block cut smooth and well fitting
> That design might cover their face . . .
> With *Usura*
> No picture is made to endure nor to live with
> But it is made to sell and sell quickly . . .
> *Usura* rusteth the chisel.
> It rusteth the craft and the craftsman,
> It gnaweth the thread in the loom.
> None learneth to weave gold in their pattern . . .
> *Usura* slayeth the child of the womb . . .
> Corpses are set to banquet at behest of *Usura*.

EZRA POUND:
Canto xlv

> From the blight of graceless consumption,
> From the deceit of advertisement,
> From death in plenty,
> From the tyranny of acquisition,
> From the bondage of the cash-nexus,
> From the compounded evils of crude interest,
> From the exploitation of our fellows,
> From the coarseness of riches,
> From the banality of wasting possession,
> From empty satedness with technology,
> From the curse of *Usura*.
> God save this people: good Lord, deliver us.   **Amen.**

They only betray themselves and realize it not. For in their
hearts there is a sickness.

Surah of The Cow, v. 9–10

Mankind is sick, the world distempered lies . . .
The wise and good like kind physicians are,
They strive to heal them by their care.
For since the sickness is (they find)
A sad distemper of the mind:
All railings they impute,
All injuries, unto the sore disease
They are expressly come to ease.

If we would to the world's distempered mind
Impute the rage which there we find,
We might . . . pity all the griefs we see,
Anointing every malady with precious oil and balm;
And while ourselves are calm,
Our art improve to rescue them . . .

But let's not fondly our own selves beguile:
If we revile 'cause they revile,
Ourselves infected with their sore disease . . .

THOMAS TRAHERNE:
Poems

Give thy saving health, O Lord, to all nations.
In the cruse of hatred there is no oil and wine
To heal the wounds of men:
No sanity in the distempers of anger and contention,
No ease for sorrows from hearts that only curse,
From wills that take the contagion they denounce,
From minds that sicken, being sickened.
Heal us, Lord, within, that we may be thy healers
In the world around. Let us bear away the malice
In the steadfast health of love, in the whole life
Of thy compassion.   Amen.

Go, my songs, to the lonely and the unsatisfied . . .
Speak against unconscious oppression,
Speak against the tyranny of the unimaginative . . .
Go to the hideously wedded,
Go to them whose failure is concealed . . .
Go in a friendly manner, go with an open speech,
Be eager to find new evils and new good.
Be against all forms of oppression.
Go to those who are thickened with middle age,
To those who have lost their interest.
Go out and defy opinion.

EZRA POUND:
Commission

Come, my soul, come in petition,
Come with all these in the caring of your spirit.
Speak with the lips of the imaginative:
Bear the unloved, the unloving,
To the compassion of God. Remember
The thwarted, the cheated, the cheating,
The drop-outs, the angry, the broken.
Set the 'So be it' of the will of God
Against 'Thus it is' of men's ill-doing, ill-shaping.

Come with open speech,
Come in the friendship of hope.
Strengthen the subtle cords
That bind the passion of peace
With the woes of the world.
In the travail of righteousness come,
Bring the lonely, the empty, the sated,
To the authority of God.

So teach us to pray.   Amen.

Petition

Are there locks upon your hearts?

Surah of Muḥammad, v. 27

'Tis love alone can hearts unlock . . .
What magic bolts, what mystic bars . . .
Maintain the will!
Disband dull fears, give faith the day.
It is love's siege and sure to be
Your triumph through his victory.
'Tis cowardice that keeps this field
And want of courage not to yield.
Yield, then, O yield, that love may win
The fort at last and let life in . . .
This fort of your fair self, if't be not won,
He is repulsed indeed, but you're undone.

RICHARD CRASHAW:
Poems

Save us, O Lord, from hardness, from barredness,
Of heart.

Let thy coming, Lord, find our compassion open,
Open to the lonely, the demanding, the uninteresting,
Open to receive, to welcome, to befriend.

Let thy coming, Lord, find our conscience open.
Open to the reproach of thy holy law,
Open to the rebuke of righteousness,
Open to ask forgiveness, open to find mercy.

Let thy coming, Lord, find our wonder open,
Open to thy signs, alerted to mystery,
Kindling to gratitude,
Open to greet with joy the benedictions of the earth.

The key thou gavest me to turn, I yield to thee.

Amen.

We beseech thee, Lord,
Remember all for good:
Have pity upon all, O sovereign Lord.

Fill our garners with all manner of store,
Preserve our marriages in peace and concord,
   Nourish our infants,
   Lead forward our youth,
   Sustain our aged,

Comfort the faint-hearted,
   Gather together the dispersed,
   Restore the wanderers,
   Set free the troubled with unclean spirits,
Travel with the travellers,
   Stand forth for the widow, Shield the orphan,
   Rescue the captive and heal the sick.

Remember, O God, all who need thy great compassion,
And upon all pour out thy rich pity.

For thou, Lord, art the succour of the succourless,
   The hope of the hopeless,
   The Saviour of the tempest-tossed,
   The harbour of the voyager,
The physician of the sick.

For thou knowest every man and his petition,
Every house and its need,
Being the God of all spirits and of all flesh.

LANCELOT ANDREWES: *Preces Privatae*

O thou who art the sufficiency of those who seek of
   thee to be sufficed.
O thou who seekest him that desires thee
O thou desire of him that seeks thee.

Invocations from *Ḥirz al-Jawsh*

A visitor from Cordoba informed me, when I asked him for news of that city, that he had seen our dwelling, that its traces were well-nigh obliterated and its waymarks effaced . . . I remembered the days I had passed in that fair mansion . . . now scattered by the hand of exile and torn to pieces by the finger of expatriation. I saw in my mind's eye the ruin of that noble house in whose midst I had grown to man's estate.

IBN ḤAZM:
The Ring of the Dove

Lord of mercy and God of the human family, you have conjoined our being and our dwelling in token of your compassion. We thank you for the love of land and landscape in our hearts, for the birthmark of home by which we know ourselves.

Remember all whose lives are broken in our time by dispossession, by homelessness and exile, who live in tented privation while others occupy their soil and farm their lands.

Arm us against the casual forgetfulness of what for others is the unforgettable, the shadowed future, the shattered past.

In your ancient law, you commanded a care for the stranger within our gates. What of our gates that make the stranger? Strangers within their own gates, embittered and undone?

Sustain with your mercy the agencies of ministry to refugees, the measures for present relief and future reconciliation. Subdue the community of nations in their passions and their policies to your righteous will that justice may come again and peace lift up her lovely face.   Amen.

Seek ye first the Kingdom of God, and his righteousness.

The Gospel according to Matthew, Chapter 6:33

O God, thou hast been gracious to men and bestowed upon them a moral awareness. It is a spirit from thee. What it enjoins and what it prohibits are alike thine. Whosoever obeys it obeys thee: he who flouts it flouts thee. Thou hast left to us the obeying of it.

Keep our doings within the bounds of this moral sense. O God, do not let us be so encumbered with the things of this world that we transgress the bounds of conscience. O God, so inspire men that they follow no other guidance. Teach them not to override it for any alternative, however impressive. Let them set up no idols to its exclusion to be worshipped or esteemed as good.

For, outside conscience, there is no good. O God, guide those who preside over human affairs that they establish no order that will oblige men to transgress conscience and that they do not inflict on others wrongs that are immediate and concrete, for the sake of something supposedly and ultimately good for society. For this is the origin of man's tragic trouble and the source of the evil within him.

O God, thou hast not endowed conscience with material force to compel from man a reluctant obedience. So grant them inwardly a spiritual compulsion in which they will follow it out of choice and delight . . . O God, guide thy servants who have gone almost irretrievably astray. Thou art the Hearer and the Answerer.

KĀMIL ḤUSSEIN:
City of Wrong

Who buys my thoughts
Buys not a cup of honey
That sweetens every taste.
He buys the throb of young Afric's soul,
The soul of teeming millions,
Hungry, naked, sick,
Yearning, pleading, waiting.

Who buys my thoughts
Buys not some false pretence
Of oracles and tin gods.
He buys the thoughts projected by the mass
Of restless youths, who are born
Into deep and clashing cultures,
Sorting, questioning, watching.

Who buys my thoughts
Buys the spirit of the age
The unquenching fire that smoulders
And smoulders
In every living heart
That is true and noble and suffering:
It burns o'er all the earth,
Destroying, chastening, cleansing.

DENNIS OSADEBAY:
Poems

Lord, hear the prayers of our thoughts,

Direct the thoughts of our prayers.

Make plain thy will,
Make sure our obedience.

In thy mercy,

Hallow, rule, teach, and renew our aspirations,
And bend our hearts to their achieving.   Amen.

Come let us now enquire
How each is faring. Let us gain—
If gain we may, upon this plain

Of trouble vast where pastures pure,
From fear secure, are not to find—
The spirit's far desire.

SHAMS AL-DĪN ḤĀFIẒ:
Wild Deer

Do not despair of the Spirit of God. It is only those who give the
lie to him who despair of the Spirit of God.

Surah of Joseph, v. 87

I pray thee, Lord, let my way be resolute and my purpose firm in
thy good counsel. Grant me, O Lord, the boon of gratefulness for
thy grace, the beauty that belongs with thy worship. Give me a
pure and reverent heart, uprightness of character, a tongue that
speaks right and deeds that are worthy, O Lord God.

ABŪ ḤAMĪD AL-GHAZĀLĪ:
The Reviving of Religion

Eternal God,
    the light of the minds that know thee,
    the joy of the hearts that love thee,
    the strength of the wills that serve thee,
Grant us
    so to know thee that we may truly love thee,
    so to love thee that we may freely serve thee,
whom to serve is perfect freedom,
    to the glory of thy holy Name.

The Gelasian Sacramentary

. . . listen
To the deep pulse of Africa beating in the
    mist of forgotten villages.
See the tired moon comes down to her bed on the
    slack sea,
The laughter grows weary, the story tellers even
Are nodding their heads like a child on the back of its
    mother.
The feet of the dancers grow heavy and heavy the
    voice of the answering choirs.
It is the hour of night, the night that dreams,
Leaning upon this hill of clouds, wrapped in its long,
    milky cloth.
The roofs of the huts gleam tenderly. What do they say
    so secretly to the stars?
Inside, the fire goes out among intimate smells, that are
    acrid and sweet.

    LÉOPOLD SÉDAR SENGHOR: *Night in Senegal*

O bless this people, Lord, who seek their own face
under the mask and can hardly recognize it . . .

O bless this people that breaks its bond . . .

And with them, all the peoples of Europe,
All the peoples of Asia,
All the peoples of Africa,
All the peoples of America,
Who sweat blood and sufferings.
And see, in the midst of these millions of waves
The sea swell of the heads of my people.
And grant to their warm hands that they may clasp
The earth in a girdle of brotherly hands,
Beneath the rainbow of thy peace.

    LÉOPOLD SÉDAR SENGHOR: *Prayer for Peace*

Active is he, day in and day out.

Surah of The All-Merciful, v. 29

His least act every day is that
                              he despatches three armies:
One from the loins of the fathers to the mothers,
In order that the seed may grow in the womb:
One army from the wombs to the earth,
That the world may be filled with male and female:
One army from the earth to what lies beyond death . . .

JALĀL AL-DĪN RŪMĪ: *Mathnawi*

Not a day passes, not a minute or second
                              without an accouchement:
Not a day passes, not a minute or second
                              without a corpse . . .
. . . and the living looking upon it.

WALT WHITMAN: *To Think of Time*

Lord, in thee we live and have our being.
Thou art he who brings to birth and brings to death.
Thou dost not weary of mankind,
But givest day by day the gift of life,
Making men and women the creators
In the tireless procession of the generations,
Fearfully and wonderfully made.
Grant us in our time the hallowing of the womb
And reverence for the mystery of life.
Teach us, in the teeming world, the due trust of birth,
To keep faith with the newly born, the yet unborn,
Lest the crowded earth shall not suffice them.
And in the midst of life, we pray for those in death,
In the ceaseless exodus of the departing.
Thine it is to summon, thine to have mercy and to save.

Amen.

O Lord, grant us in our wives and in our offspring the joy of our eyes.

Surah of Salvation, v. 74

God that mad'st her well regard her,
How she is so fair and bonny.
From here to there to the sea's border
Dame or damsel there's not any
Hath of perfect charms so many.
Thoughts of her are of dream's order.
God that mad'st her well regard her.

EZRA POUND:
Dieu Qui L'a Faicte

We are delighted with the new arrival. God give him a large share of his name and the utmost of that after which he is called . . . It is fortunate for one who arrives into this world with the spring smiling on his face, bidding him welcome with its roses and its flowers, presenting him with its rich verdure . . . I ought not indeed to congratulate . . . but joy overcame me and made me indiscreet.

ABŪ-L-ʿALĀ AL-MAʿARĪ:
Letters

Lord, grant us joy of our wives and children. Make reverence the garment of our love and hallowing the benediction of our homes. By the surety of the troth we keep make safe the troths of all. For the joy of our eyes grant us faith in our souls. Make us and ours ready for all seasons, gay and grave. Make our loves true and in their truth make our nation glad.

Lord, hear our prayer: our prayer, Lord, hear. Amen.

God knows that my wood produces no fire . . . (yet) there is no
question that our hearts meet in affection, and that our spirits
shake hands every day, nay, every hour.

The bonds of our loves, Lord, hallow and enrich.

I have been awaiting intelligence of you as the traveller who has
lagged behind the caravan asks where his comrades are gone, or
the pasture-hunter enquires where the rain has fallen.

The cares of our loves, Lord, hallow and direct.

I can only hope that the shell of your fortune may produce a
pearl of rare price and that the buds of your times may open into
the sweetest flower.

The hopes of our loves, Lord, hallow and fulfil.

I beg you will not drive your reed over an answer to this letter,
for I know so well what is in your mind that I need not give
trouble to your hand. God who is Almighty will protect you . . .
and may the rising sun each morning bring you recruited strength

The pledges of our loves, Lord, hallow and renew.

I shall preserve my affection for you as the rhyming syllable is
preserved from alteration of vowel or consonant . . . For our love
is in a well-guarded place, secure against time's ravages.

The love of our loves, Lord, keep in thy truth.

ABŪ-L-ʿALĀ AL-MAʿARĪ
Greetings in his *Letter.*

In God's Name be the course and the mooring. Embark.

Surah of Hūd, v. 41

> Give us thy wisdom
> More than ever before,
> Now that our country
> Has passed the door
> To wider freedom.
>
> Hold a people's hand
> And give us thy heart,
> So that every man lives in the land,
> And holds dear the part
> He must play,
> To fulfil this day.
>
> Give us thy glory,
> In the days ahead,
> O let our country be proud of its story
> When we are dead.

GEORGE CAMPBELL:
Jamaica Constitution Day Poem

Remember, O Lord, in thy mercy this people, and all peoples, this land and every land.

Look graciously upon the youth in the venture of life's prospect and upon the aged in the anchorage of days.

Remember those in the full tide of their affairs—rulers, leaders, artists, teachers, doctors, captains of industry and makers of science, and all whose well-being they carry in their trust.

Remember in thy compassion all travellers and wayfarers, all pilgrims and passengers, and every common man preserve thou, in his going out and coming in, his living and his dying, O merciful Lord.   Amen.

L

It is as one soul he created you, and as one soul he gives you life.

Surah of Luqmān, v. 27

Our bread and water are of one table:
The progeny of Adam are as a single soul.

MUḤAMMAD IQBĀL:
Jāvid Nāma

Holy be the white head of a negro,
Sacred be the black flax of a black child.
Holy be the golden down
That will stream in the waves of the wind
And will thin like dispersing cloud.
Holy be heads of Chinese hair,
Sea calm sea impersonal
Deep flowering of the mellow and traditional.
Heads of peoples fair
Bright shimmering from the riches of their species:
Heads of Indians
With feeling of distance and space and dusk:
Heads of wheaten gold,
Heads of peoples dark
So strong, so original,
All of the earth and the sun.

GEORGE CAMPBELL:
Holy

Surely you know that you are God's temple, where the Spirit of
God dwells. Anyone who destroys God's temple will be himself
destroyed by God. For the temple of God is holy, and that temple
you are.

The First Epistle to the Corinthians, Chapter 3:16–17

Lord, teach us to hallow our humanity in the hallowing of thy
Name.   Amen.

O man, who has beguiled you away from your kindly Lord, who
created you and fashioned you, wrought you with such symmetry
and ordered you as he willed the design?

Surah of The Cataclysm, v. 6–8

Here, Lord, before you tonight are the bodies of
sleeping men:

> The pure body of the tiny child,
> The soiled body of the prostitute,
> The vigorous body of the athlete,
> The exhausted body of the factory worker,
> The soft body of the playboy,
> The surfeited body of the rich man,
> The starved body of the poor man,
> The painful body of the injured man,
> The paralysed body of the cripple,
> All bodies, Lord, of all ages.

I offer them all to you, Lord, and ask you to bless them,
While they lie in silence, wrapped in your night.
Left by their sleeping souls,
They are there before your eyes, your own.
Tomorrow, shaken from their sleep,
They will have to resume their work.
May they be servants and not masters,
Welcoming homes and not prisons,
Temples of the living God and not tombs.
May these bodies be developed, purified, transfigured,
By those who dwell in them.

MICHEL QUOIST:
The Pornographic Magazine in Prayers of Life

They conceal themselves from men, but not from God. For he is with them the while they muse aloud with themselves by night in his despite. God is there encompassing all they do.

Whoever does evil and wrongs himself and then prays God's forgiveness will find that God is All-forgiving and All-merciful.

Surah of Women, v. 108, 110

The drowsy street eyes me,
And the brick walls bid me refrain,
And I sense God, too, watching me,
The night and the lamp—they are noting me,
And the star—why does the star
Want to beckon me so
Just when I am falling into sordid shame?
What am I but a body-slave?
The shame is like poison in my frame:
I feel the toxic evil overpowering me.
'Tis not the murmuring of the night transporting me,
Nor am I inebriate in the whispering air,
Nor can I tax some bewitching humming in the moonlight,
That I sense my inmost self inside a shroud.

HILĀL NĀJĪ:
The Worshipper of the Flesh

Sell not yourself at a little price, being so precious in God's eyes.

JALĀL AL-DĪN RŪMĪ:
Discourses

In your watchful compassion, Lord, guard and guide us. Amen.

> Have we not given him two eyes?
>
> Surah of The Land, v. 8

Thank you, Lord, for my eyes
    Windows open on the wide world . . .
May my look never be one of disappointment,
Disillusionment, despair;
But may it know how to admire, contemplate, adore.

May my gaze not soil the one it touches,
May it not disturb, but may it bring peace.
May it not sadden, but rather may it transmit joy.
May it not attract to hold captive,
But rather may it persuade others
To rise above themselves to you.

I give you my soul,
I give you my body,
I give you my eyes,
That, in looking at men, my brothers,
It may be you who look at them,
And you who beckon.

MICHEL QUOIST:
Eyes in *Prayers of Life*

Tell me, what have my eyes seen?
Why have they demented been?
Hot like the oven burn mine eyes.
Remembrance in them restless lies.
They went upon their obstinate way,
Where in their waiting troubles lay.

SHĀH ʿABDUL LAṬĪF:
Obstinate Eyes, in *Sindhi Poems*

God be in my eyes and in my looking.

O man, you are making your toilsome way unto your Lord, to find what you have wrought.

Stage after stage you will surely ride.

Surah of The Rending, v. 6, 19

The swaying coach, for all its load,
   Runs lightly as it rocks:
Grey time goes driving down the road,
   Nor ever leaves the box.

We jump into the coach at dawn,
   Alert and fresh and free,
And holding broken bones in scorn,
   'Go on!' shout we.

By midday all is changed about,
   Our morning hearts are cool:
We fear the slow descents and shout:
   'Go slow! you fool!'

By dusk we're used to jolt and din,
   And when the light is gone
We sleep before we reach the inn,
   As time drives on.

ALEXANDER PUSHKIN:
The Coach of Life

Lord of men, who givest life and bringest to death, thou art the beginning and the end, the First and the Last, unchanging in every scene.

Keep us this and every day, in the path of life. Grant us strength according to our time. Unite our days in one. Let thy compassion go before and follow after us, that in the entail of our lives we may find the proof of thy mercy. For unto thee is our becoming and our returning. Amen.

He gives life and he makes to die and to him you shall be returned.

Surah of Jonah, v. 57

> See! they return: Ah! see the tentative
> Movements and the slow feet,
> The trouble in the pace and the uncertain
> Wavering.
> See! they return, one and by one,
> With fear, as half awakened,
> As if the snow should hesitate
> And murmur in the wind,
> And half turn back.

EZRA POUND:
The Return

Finally, there is the separation that is caused by death, that final parting . . . Here all tongues are baffled: the cord of every remedy is severed. No other course remains open but patient fortitude . . .

IBN ḤAZM:
The Ring of the Dove

To you, Lord, is entrusted all that we have and are—our salvation, our vocation, our daily work, our families, our life and our death. So at the end, Lord, our prayer is the sum of all desire and of all prayer. Take and receive, Lord, my whole freedom, my memory, my understanding and my whole will, all that I have and possess. From you it came, Lord, to you I offer it all again. All is yours, dispose of it entirely according to your will. Give me only your love and your grace, for that is enough.

KARL RAHNER:
Prayers for Meditation

Holy the God of the angels:
> he has wrought the resurrection.

Holy the God of the prophets:
> he has wrought the redemption.

Holy the God of the apostles:
> he has wrought forgiveness.

Corpus Inscriptionum Latinarum

O God, have mercy on me when I die
And lie lonely in the grave,
And when I stand between your hands;
For I have been a stranger in the world.

Pilgrimage Prayers

O God, give him rest with the devout and the just,
In the place of the pasture of rest
And of refreshment, of waters in the paradise
Of delight, whence grief and pain and sighing
Have fled away.
Holy, holy, holy, Lord God of hosts,
Heaven and earth are full of your holy glory.

Egyptian Commendation, 5th century

May he be with God,
May he be with the living God,
May he be with the immortal God,
May he be in the righteousness of God,
May he be in the hands of God,
May he be in the great Name of God,
May he be where God's greatness is,
May he live in God, now and in the day
Of judgment, and in the eternal life of heaven.

Monumenta Ecclesiae Liturgica

God be at my end and at my departing.

Lord God, here is a new creation. Open it to me in thy obedience
and close it for me in thy forgiveness and thy favour. Provide for
me herein a goodness thou mayest find acceptable at my hands.
Let it be to me pure and prosperous and whatsoever of evil I do
in it do thou pardon me therein, for thou art ever forgiving and
merciful, loving and kindly.

ABŪ ḤAMID AL-GHAZĀLĪ:
The Reviving of Religion, 'Morning Prayer of Abraham'

Keep me in thy love
As thou wouldest that all should be kept
      in mine.
May everything in this my being
Be directed to thy glory
And may I never despair.
For I am under thy hand,
And in thee is all power and goodness.

DAG HAMMARSKJÖLD:
Markings

Be thou my vision, O Lord of my heart:
Nought be all else to me save that thou art,
Thou my whole thought, by day or by night,
Waking or sleeping, thy presence my light.

Be thou my wisdom, thou my true word,
I ever with thee and thou with me, Lord . . .
Thou and thou only first in my heart,
High King of Heaven, my treasure thou art.
Heart of my own heart, whatever befall,
Still be my vision, O Ruler of all.

An ancient Irish Prayer

Lord our God, to thee does man call in the day of his need: thee does he thank in times of joy. Thou art everywhere present. Thou art near where thy community is gathered together.

Some perhaps flying from heavy thoughts, or followed by heavy thoughts. But some, too, coming from a quiet life of contentment and some perhaps with a satisfied longing hidden in a thankful heart enveloped in joyous thoughts.

Yet all drawn by the desire to seek God, the Friend of the thankful in blessed trust, the consolation of the weak in strengthening communion, the refuge of the anxious in secret comfort. . . .

So let thy self be found in this hour . . . that the happy may find courage to rejoice at thy good gifts, that the sorrowful may find courage to accept thy perfect gifts.

For to men there is a difference in these things, the difference of joy and sorrow. But for thee, O Lord, there is no difference: everything that comes from thee is a good and perfect gift.

SØREN KIERKEGAARD:
Prayers

Petitions terminate in the presence of his bounty: needs fade away as the soul finds her reliance in himself. The need of the creature is not satisfied by the whole of created things. Rather his infinite longing demands to be met by infinite graciousness and power, by none other than the truth himself, praised and exalted be he.

FAKHR AL-DĪN AL-RĀZĪ:
The Clear and the Shining

NOTES ON AUTHORS
SOURCES
INDEXES

Notes on Authors

As we have drawn on obscurity as well as fame, these paragraphs are not inclusive. Other names will be found in the Index. Dates of Muslims are given here according to the Islamic calendar which begins in A.D. 622 with Muḥammad's emigration from Mecca to Medina, which was 'the year of the Hijrah', or *Anno Hegirae*, hence the letters A.H. To facilitate recognition for those unfamiliar with the Hijrah Calendar the western century is added in brackets.

SHĀH 'ABDUL LAṬĪF, *1091–1161 A.H. (18th century)*

A village poet and saint of Sindh, whose *Shahju Risālo* is highly esteemed in Sindhi Islam as a work of great literary power and religious authority. He drew on the popular stories of local minstrels and transformed them into the vehicles of spiritual parable and praise.

LANCELOT ANDREWES, *A.D. 1555–1626*

Bishop of Winchester, England. His Latin book of personal devotions, *Preces Privatae*, was never intended for the public eye. But its ripe Biblical learning and warm fervour have enriched the prayers of many in the generations since his day.

AUGUSTINE OF HIPPO, *A.D. 354–440*

Great Christian saint, bishop and theologian, whose autobiography, *The Confessions*, is a classic of personal, spiritual revolution, the narrative of a man 'lost enough to be found' by faith. His *City of God*, his Sermons and Commentaries, deeply moulded Christian thought through the middle centuries.

ʿABD AL-LAṬĪF AL-BAGHDĀDĪ, *557–629 A.H.* (*12/13th centuries*)

A most notable Islamic philosopher and scientist, who taught in Baghdad and travelled in Greece, Turkey, and Egypt. He was held in great esteem by Salāḥ al-Dīn (Saladin), whose camp he joined outside Acre. He excelled in medical skill and his travelogue contains a graphic description of plague in Cairo.

MUṢṬAFĀ AL-BAKRĪ, *1099–1162 A.H.* (*18th century*)

Born at Damascus in the year John Bunyan died in Bedford, Al-Bakrī lived in Ottoman Palestine and in Cairo and Istanbul. He was a government official and a practising Ṣūfī. His first manual of prayers was composed in Jerusalem. Known as 'the ascetic traveller', his devotional writing was widely influential in the Arab world.

ABUBAKAR TAFAWA BALEWA, *1331–1385 A.H.* (*20th century*)

Born at Bauchi in Northern Nigeria, a teacher and a statesman and first Federal Premier of Nigeria, he died at the hands of assassins in the coup of January 1966. His novel, *Shaihu Umar*, vividly depicts the Hausa world of seventy years ago and its single-minded piety and the harsh realities of trans-Saharan travel.

ALEXANDER A. BLOK, *A.D. 1880–1921*

A very prominent poet in his generation in Russia, his verses are laden with carnal emotion and mystical melody, representing what one admirer called 'the tragic tenour of the era'.

THOMAS BRADWARDINE, *c. A.D. 1290–1349*

Linked by Geoffrey Chaucer (in *The Canterbury Tales*) with Augustine and Boethius, Bradwardine enjoyed great repute as a theologian before his election as Archbishop of Canterbury in

1349. He died within seven days of landing at Dover to take up his charge. The Black Death was raging in England when he crossed the Channel.

BERTOLT BRECHT, *A.D. 1898–1956*

German playwright with a strong revolutionary and didactic passion. In his plays he aims to preclude identification or sympathy with his characters on the part of the audience, in order to compel the spectator to reach a verdict about the miseries and paradoxes he witnesses, the empty conventions and social follies.

JOHN BUNYAN, *A.D. 1628–1688*

Author of *The Pilgrim's Progress* and *Grace Abounding* and one of the finest, lowliest figures in English Christian tradition, a man of simple greatness, telling imagination, warm compassion and vivid speech. His place in literature is truly 'an exaltation of the humble and meek'.

ALBERT CAMUS, *A.D. 1913–1960*

A French Algerian novelist and playwright with a buoyant capacity for life, for sunshine and the senses, and a thoroughgoing quality of ultimate despair about it. His literary works reflect with great force and clarity of language the wretchedness and tragedy of the human condition, its hypocrisy, its pathos and its pointless, but still persistent, demand for meaning.

GEORGE CAMPBELL

A Jamaican poet whose *First Poems* were published in Kingston in 1945, and a voice of sanity, gentleness, and aspiration in the stresses and changes of the Caribbean world.

CLEMENT OF ROME, *died c. A.D. 100*

Bishop of Rome near the close of the first Christian century and author of the *Epistle to the Corinthians*, one of the important documents of the early Church after the writings of the New Testament. It has been conjectured that Clement is the person of that name to whom Paul refers in his *Epistle to the Philippians* (Chapter 4:3).

ARTHUR HUGH CLOUGH, *A.D. 1819–1861*

An English poet, the favourite pupil at Rugby School of the famous Thomas Arnold, and a close friend of his son, Matthew, Clough's poems reflect the alert, and often burdened, spirit with which he sensed and satirized the hypocrisies of his time.

STEPHEN CRANE, *A.D. 1871–1900*

The son of a Methodist minister in New Jersey, Crane struggled with poverty and ill-health as a journalist in New York, and as a war correspondent. He settled in England but illness, stemming from his privations, cut short his life. Dying before the age of thirty, he left stories and poems with a grimly realist quality of pathos and irony.

THOMAS CRANMER, *A.D. 1489–1556*

A scholarly figure, oddly yet heroically present at the centre of the stage through the tumult of the English Reformation. His external career as Archbishop of Canterbury ended in brokenness and despair in the reign of Mary. But finding God again beyond the God he had lost, he recanted his recantation and in death gave to the English Church a sign of courage as hauntingly eloquent as his English *Litany*.

RICHARD CRASHAW, *c. A.D. 1613–1649*

Religious poet of seventeenth-century England, born of Puritan stock and converted to the Roman Catholic Church some few years before his death. He wrote sacred verse in both English and Latin, with an artistry of phrase and fervour of devotion unexcelled in an age of deep religious feelings and political passion.

'ABD AL- 'AZĪZ AL-DĪRĪNĪ, *died c. 697 A.H.* (*13th century*)

A celebrated poet and Ṣūfī master who lived in rural Egypt and commented on the Qur'ān, notably the *Fātiḥah*, and reputedly wrote a work with the title: *Gathered Pearls on Assorted Questions.*

JOHN DONNE, *A.D. 1572–1631*

The most memorable English preacher of the seventeenth, and perhaps of any, century was first 'Jack' Donne, a gay, amorous poet. The intensity of his religious experience, his sense of evil, of judgment and of death, his grasp on grace and redemption, were tuned to a fine and sombre eloquence by his wide erudition, his power of imagery and his probing wit. And still, because of him, 'love's mysteries in souls do grow'.

FRANCIS OF ASSISI, *A.D. 1181–1226*

Son of a rich clothier in Assisi, Italy, Francis 'learned Christ' through a crisis of compassion in which he embraced poverty and found its positive meaning in active love and Gospel preaching. His repair of a ruined church became the symbol and the magnet of a discipleship which grew into the Franciscan Order. Seven years before his death he visited the Arab East. He lives in history in the 'sign' of the five wounds, the *Stigmata*.

ALEKSEI K. GASTEV, *A.D. 1882–1941*

One of a group of young proletarian poets in Russia who wrote ecstatically of the power of the machine and celebrated the promise of collectivism and new industrialization. He thought the universe a huge foundry.

M

PAULUS GERHARDT, *c. A.D. 1607–1676*

One of the finest poets of German Lutheran Christianity, who drew upon medieval sources and upon an ardent love of nature and sense of grace to give hymns of rich devotion to the music of Christian worship.

ABŪ ḤAMĪD MUḤAMMAD AL-GHAZĀLĪ, *450–505 A.H.*
(11th century)

The most justly famous of spiritual leaders in Islam. While in his thirties and already a successful philosopher, he experienced a deep, personal crisis of conversion from pride and despair. His masterpiece, *Iḥyā' Ulūm al-Dīn* (lit. 'The Reviving of the Sciences of Religion'), is a profound work of intellectual range and moral perception and embraces knowledge, evil, sin, temptation, discipline, sanctity, and hope, among its themes. Other numerous works gave wide currency to his legacy as a supreme exponent of Islamic existence.

SHAMS AL-DĪN ḤĀFIẒ, *720–791 A.H. (14th century)*

Foremost in the art of Persian *ghazal* poetry, Ḥāfiẓ, born in Shirāz—the city of poets—and a Shī'ah Muslim (his name indicates that he had learned the Qur'ān by heart), lived through chequered times. 'What is this anarchy that I see in the lunatic world?' he wrote. Beneath the dismaying tumults, his poems breathe a tranquillity of soul of which an English translator said: 'They are the plants and flowers of light; they toil not, neither do they spin, yet eternity is full of their glory.'

ḤAFṢA OF GRANADA, *c. 530–586 A.H. (12th century)*

Celebrated poetess in Spain in the days of the Almoravids, Ḥafṣa Bint al-Ḥajj was a woman of great social charm whose Arabic verses were characterized by a simple directness and human sympathy. She lived through a devastating plague at Marrakesh, Morocco, which left a deep mark upon her courtly mind. She died there some years later.

DAG HAMMARSKJÖLD, *A.D. 1905–1961*

'A man of true inner greatness in a position of high leadership . . . sustained and inspired by pure and firmly founded beliefs and ideals about life and relationships . . . a very brilliant, orderly, pragmatic and subtle mind.' Second Secretary-General of the United Nations, a man of peace and prayer.[1]

AMĪR HAMZAH, *1329–1365 A.H.* (*20th century*)

A Malayan prince, writing in Bahasa Indonesian, his poems breathe a deep wistfulness for human love and speak an ardent Muslim devotion. His two volumes of verse were: *Songs of Loneliness* and *Fruits of Longing*. He edited other poems called *License from the East* and was fluent in Persian, Urdu, and Turkish. He was killed by revolutionaries in Sumatra.

JOHN S. HOYLAND, *born 1887*

A Christian educator who devoted many years in India and laboured to interpret India to the West and Christ to India. He wrote the biographies of G. K. Gokhale and C. F. Andrews and translated Mahatma Gandhi's *Songs from Prison* into English. He also wrote *The Great Forerunner*, a study of the relation of Platonism to Christianity.

KĀMIL ḤUSSEIN, *born 1320 A.H.* (*20th century*)

Cairo surgeon and educationalist, whose contemporary reflections on the philosophy of religion, archaeology, psychology, and Arabic literature have found expression in essays and other works, notably *Qaryah Ẓālimah* (City of Wrong), a study of the motives and decisions leading up to the rejection of Jesus in the first century, as symptomatic of the whole range of evil in human society.

[1] Quoted from the Introduction to Dag Hammarskjöld: *The Servant of Peace, A Selection of his Speeches*, edited by W. Foote, London, 1962, pp. 13–14.

ABŪ MUḤAMMAD ʿALĪ IBN ḤAZM, *384–456 A.H.*
(11th century)

Celebrated theologian and legist of Cordoba and a doughty
controversialist who lived through turbulent times of political
unrest and confronted them with a sharp and prolific pen. His
treatise on the art and practice of love, *The Ring of the Dove*, is in
quieter vein and remains one of the most fascinating literary
legacies of Muslim Spain.

AḤMAD IBN IDRĪS, *d. 1253 A.H. (early 19th century)*

A noted Moroccan mystic who migrated, first to Cairo and then
to Mecca, and attracted a large following of disciples. His
theology hardened in his later years and he died in ʿAsīr, under
the protection of the Wahhābī rulers. His influence survives
among the Sanūsiyyah of Libya and in the Sudan.

ʿIYĀD IBN MŪSĀ, *476–544 A.H. (11th century)*

Moroccan poet and historian, born at Ceuta, who became Qāḍī of
Cordoba and died in Marrakesh. He wrote extensively in the
field of Tradition and Mālikite law.

ABŪ BAKR MUḤAMMAD IBN TUFAYL, *c. 505–581 A.H.*
(12th century)

A native of Granada, Spain, and an official of the Almohad court
in Cordoba. His major work was a philosophical romance, in
which a desert island 'Crusoe' ripened, as he grew in years, in the
steady apprehension of rational truth, though entirely cut off from
all human intercourse. When Islam reached his island he was
convinced of its utter accord with philosophy. He initiated a
mission to convert the world, but abandoned the venture to retire
to his island sanctuary of pure belief and philosophic calm.

EUGENE IONESCO, *born 1912*

A dramatist of French Rumanian parentage who preaches the evils of conformism and satirizes, with sometimes witty and always mordant irony, what he considers to be the banalities of society, sex, and friendship, intimating his view of the emptiness and oppressiveness of the human scene.

MUḤAMMAD IQBĀL, *1294–1357 A.H.* (*20th century*)

The greatest literary figure in twentieth-century Islam in Asia. His poems in Persian and Urdu contributed massively to the renewal of Muslim vitality in the sub-continent of India. He is revered by multitudes as the spiritual mainspring of Pakistan. He had a lively sympathy with such western thinkers as Nietzsche, Shaw, and Bergson.

ʿABD AL-QĀDIR AL-JĪLĀNĪ, *470–561 A.H.* (*12th century*)

A distinguished jurist of the Ḥanbalī School, who became a celebrated preacher, after an experience of Ṣūfī illumination in Baghdad when he was almost fifty years of age. He originated the Qādiriyyah Order, which spread widely in western Asia, Egypt and, later, India. Its litanies and prayer manuals direct the devotional life of initiates and 'lay' associates.

SØREN KIERKEGAARD, *A.D. 1813–1855*

One of the foremost influences from the nineteenth century in contemporary Christian thought. His early death symbolizes the strain of sadness which beset his family and his career. His incisive mind at length found its authentic 'word' in existential faith and in a passionate rejection of institutional religion. Nevertheless his meditations on 'Holy Communion' represent his most intense message to posterity in their discovery of grace.

HUGH LATIMER, *c. A.D. 1485–1555*

Bishop of Worcester, England, and with Nicholas Ridley and Thomas Cranmer, the most famous martyr of the English Reformation. He was a forceful and lively preacher whose robust personality surmounted the pathos of his old age and his tragic end.

ABŪ-L-ᶜALĀ AL-MAᶜARĪ, *363–449 A.H. (10/11th centuries)*

A leading poet and thinker and one of the profoundest sceptics within Islam, a man with a wistful sense of the human tragedy. Blinded, scarred by smallpox, disillusioned with Baghdadi scholarship, he lived in seclusion near Aleppo and wrote poems, letters, and imaginative works, and through his more than eighty years he defiantly endured, yet contrived also to grace, the human enigma.

CLAUDE MCKAY, *A.D. 1889–1948*

A poet of Jamaica and America who also made extended visits to France and Russia, knew the attraction of Communism but found no rest in its dogmatics. He wrote novels of the sordid city and gentle poems of affection for a Jamaica to which he never returned.

> 'Adventure-seasoned and storm-buffeted
> I shun all signs of anchorage.'

JOHN MILTON, *A.D. 1608–1674*

'My adventurous song'—as he called it—the twelve books of *Paradise Lost* constitute a supreme achievement of English religious verse. A pastoral poet in youth, Milton lived through years of tumult and controversy. Broken and blind, he turned in old age to the tragedy of *Samson Agonistes*, 'eyeless in Gaza', a work in which the 'calm of mind' of the classic Greek theatre strangely blended with the celebration of Hebrew confidence in Divine vindication.

THE NAQSHABANDĪ ORDER

A group of Ṣūfī fraternities, founded in Persia and Bukhara by Bahā' al-Dīn Naqshabandī, who died in 791 A.H. (A.D. 1389). One of its characteristics is the practice of the recollection of God in the act of inhaling and exhaling of breath. Its liturgies contain a wealth of aspiration, contrition, and the seeking of Divine forgiveness.

EZRA POUND, *born 1885*

An American poet with a troubled history of political and literary vagaries but no less, for that reason, a voice of contemporary humanity. His *Cantos* contain passages of haunting eloquence and passionate feeling.

ALEXANDER S. PUSHKIN, *A.D. 1799–1837*

Russia's greatest poet, of partly Ethiopian descent, of which he was very proud. He lived and died in the society so vividly depicted in Tolstoy's *War and Peace*. His untimely death only added to the appeal of his genius.

MICHEL QUOIST, *born 1918*

A priest of the Roman Catholic Church whose *Prayers of Life* have had a wide circulation as a quickening example of reflective praying within the realities of the contemporary world.

KARL RAHNER, *born 1904*

One of the most influential of present-day theologians in the Roman Catholic Church, who has contributed powerfully to an interpretation of the pastoral role of the Church, as well as to inter-religious relations of Christian faith in the secular situation. He became a Jesuit in 1922 and is Professor of Christian Thought at the University of Munich, Germany.

FAKHR AL-DĪN RĀZĪ, *543–606 A.H.* (*12th century*)

Among the foremost of classical commentators on the Qur'ān, a native of Rayy (Teheran), who wrote extensively in Islamic philosophy and theology and proved a prodigious champion of his Sunnī faith. He travelled in Bukhara and beyond to India and died in Afghanistan. One of his largest works is a treatise on the Divine Names.

JALĀL AL-DĪN RŪMĪ, *604–671 A.H.* (*13th century*)

The greatest of the mystical poets of Persian Islam. Born at Balkh, he fled before the Mongol invasions to Baghdad and later to Konya in Turkey, where he became a master of Ṣūfī devotion and wrote the *Mathnawī*, the supreme classic of the Mawlawiyyah Order and a work of spiritual genius. The devotional occasions of his Order utilize the *nay*, or musical flute, and the celebrated 'whirling' rhythm.

MUṢLIḤ AL-DĪN SAʿDĪ, *c. 615–691 A.H.* (*13th century*)

The Persian poet, whose *Bustān* and *Gulistān*, written in Shirāz, the home of poets, are the pride of Persian literature. Saʿdī lived in the tragic century of Mongol expansion and the end of the ʿAbbāsid Caliphate in the sack of Baghdad (A.D. 1258). He spent much of his life in seclusion. His work is sometimes commonplace and his prose anecdotal, but his lyrics have a superb quality of simplicity and grace.

LÉOPOLD SÉDAR SENGHOR, *born 1906*

Born in a coastal village of Senegal, West Africa, now President of the Republic of Senegal and one of the most expressive of African poets in the French language. He is a mainspring of the concept of *négritude*, and the positive assertion of the African identity, while being thoroughly alive in the European idiom. His poems, *Prayer for Peace* and *Paris under Snow*, accuse, forgive, and transcend the imperial wrongs.

CHRISTOPHER SMART, *A.D. 1722–1771*

A strange paradox of a man who lived a life of tragic sordidness, of debt, insanity, and literary job-work and yet produced poems among the greatest in the lyrical, religious tradition of the English language, with an intensity of perception into nature and the skill of a miniaturist in words.

HENRY SUSO, *c. A.D. 1295–1366*

'Servant of the Eternal Wisdom', a man of German birth and a pupil of Meister Eckhart and a Dominican mystic, his meditations deeply influenced Thomas à Kempis in the *Imitation of Christ*.

GERHARDT TERSTEEGEN, *A.D. 1697–1769*

A notable hymn writer in the quietist tradition of German piety, who exercised a wide influence comparable to that of a Ṣūfī *walī* in Islam, in the fostering of spiritual devotion by a pattern of ascetic discipline. His community at Otterbeck formed the nucleus of his ideals and his poetry has been much translated.

AḤMAD AL-TĪJĀNĪ, *1150–1231 A.H. (18th century)*

A leading figure in North African Islamic religion, who studied in the great University at Fez, where he established the Ṣūfī fraternity that spread throughout the Maghrib and the Sahara, as well as Northern Nigeria and the Sudan. His prayer manuals have a still wider acceptance as a school of Muslim devotion.

THOMAS TRAHERNE, *A.D. 1637–1674*

Centuries of Meditations and the *Poems* reflect a rare quality of spiritual reverence and delight in Divine mercy. The former remained in private manuscript for three hundred years and by its publication in 1908 one of the sweetest voices of the seventeenth century emerged to bless the twentieth.

FYODOR I. TYUTCHEV, *A.D. 1803-1873*

A lyrical poet whose Russian verse, some in translation, has had a greater circulation since his death than in his own generation. His external success in the diplomatic and state service of the Czar makes a paradoxical background for a poetry that explores the dark areas of human experience.

ERIC MILNER WHITE, *A.D. 1884-1964*

For many years Dean of York Minster, England, author of *My God, my Glory* and other writings of Christian devotion, who stands in a long tradition of the care of stone, of music and of poetry, in the service of God's worship and praise.

WALT WHITMAN, *A.D. 1819-1892*

Poet of Long Island, New York, of warm human sympathies and eccentric ways, a lover of sea and soil and cities, a visionary capable of majestic poetic rhythms as well as of much sentimental egotism, he grew to become in reputation and in retrospect a voice of idealism and the American dream.

WILLIAM B. YEATS, *A.D. 1865-1939*

Dublin poet and dramatist, interpreter of Irish feeling and thought, often disillusioned with his native land but always capable of direct and vigorous expression, intense both in loves and hatreds.

ZUHAIR *'in the days of the* Jāhiliyyah' *(7th century)*

One of the outstanding poets of the 'time of ignorance' as the period before the rise of Islam is traditionally called. The precise date of Zuhair and other singers, in relation to Islam, has been a matter of controversy, some scholars believing that their poems, as they now stand, bear evidence of Islamic influence. Whether wholly prior to the Prophet or not, they celebrate both the prowess and the tragedy of the feuding tribes.

Sources

All passages quoted from the Qur'ān and, unless otherwise indicated, those from other sources, are translated by the Editor. Arabic sources not detailed are prayer manuals which exist in numerous editions, popularly reprinted in many cities, often without page numbering and usually undated. Prayers for which no source is given are by the Editor.

page

57 The Song of the Reed: Jalāl al-Dīn Rūmī, *Mathnawī*, trans. R. A. Nicholson, in *Rūmī, Poet and Mystic* (London, Allen and Unwin, 1950) p. 31.

PRAISE

60 E. Milner White, *My God, My Glory* (London, S.P.C.K., 1967) p. 112.

60 Jalāl al-Dīn Rūmī, *Discourses*, trans. A. J. Arberry (London, John Murray, 1961) p. 152.

61 Romans 11:33-6 (AV/KJV).

61 Abū-l-Salt, 'Bounty', in *Moorish Poetry*, trans. A. J. Arberry (Cambridge University Press, 1953) p. 16.

61 Revelation 15:3-4 (AV/KJV).

62 Augustine, *Confessions* I.i, trans. E. B. Pusey (London, Grant Richards, 1900) p. 1.

62 1 Timothy 1:17 (AV/KJV).

63 Karl Rahner, *Prayers for Meditation*, trans. Rosaleen Brennan (New York, Herder and Herder, 1968; London, Burns and Oates) p. 12.

page

63 Thomas Traherne, *Thanksgivings for the Body*, in *Centuries, Poems, and Thanksgivings*, ed. H. M. Margoliouth (Oxford, Clarendon Press, 1958) vol. ii, p. 228.

64 Raḥmān Bābā, 'A Pushtu Poem', in *Presenting Pakistani Poetry*, trans. Muhammad Aziz Kahn, ed. G. Allama (Karachi, Pakistan Writers' Guild, 1961) pp. 124–5.

65 Luke 1:50, 52, 53.

65 *Ramaḍān Prayers*, in *Mukhtaṣar Adʿiyat Ramaḍān* (Sidon, Lebanon, 1930).

66 Muṣṭafā al-Bakrī, 'Seal of the Five Prayers', trans. C. E. Padwick, in *Muslim Devotions* (London, S.P.C.K., 1961) p. 74.

66 Saʿdī, *The Gulistān*, trans. Edward Rehatsek (London, Allen and Unwin, 1964) p. 57.

67 *Benedicite* (*Book of Common Prayer*, Morning Prayer, from Song of the Three Children (Apocrypha) verses 35 ff.; here quoted: 35, 53, 54, 60, 63, 65).

68 'Lo! God is here, let us adore', G. Tersteegen, trans. John Wesley (*English Hymnal*, No. 637, and other books).

68 Amīr Hamzah, 'One Alone', trans. A. H. Johns, in *Malayan and Indonesian Studies*, ed. John Bastin and R. Roolvink (London, Oxford University Press, 1964) pp. 318–19.

68 ʿAbd al-Qādir al-Jīlānī, 'Wells of Prayer', trans. C. E. Padwick in *Muslim Devotions*, op. cit., p. 98.

69 *Augustine*, Confessions X. vi, op. cit., p. 234.

69 Lancelot Andrewes, *Preces Privatae*, in *Lancelot Andrewes and his Private Devotions*, ed. Alexander Whyte (London, Oliphant, Anderson and Ferrier, 1896) p. 66.

70 *Apostolic Constitutions*, Book VIII, in *Early Christian Prayers*, trans. W. Mitchell, ed. Adalbert Hamman (London, Longmans, Green and Co. Ltd., 1961) p. 105.

70 *Prayers of the Naqshabandi Order*.

page

71 Abū Ḥamīd al-Ghazālī, 'The Beginning of Guidance', trans. W. Montgomery Watt in *The Faith and Practice of Al-Ghazālī* (London, Allen and Unwin, 1953) p. 102.

71 Lancelot Andrewes, *Preces Privatae*, in *Lancelot Andrewes and his Private Devotions*, op. cit., pp. 70–1.

72 *Apostolic Constitutions* Book VIII, in *Early Christian Prayers*, op. cit., p. 113.

72 Ḥafṣa of Granada, 'The Shield', in *Moorish Poetry*, trans. A. J. Arberry, op. cit., p. 94.

73 Thomas Bradwardine, Archbishop of Canterbury, Tomb Inscription, Canterbury Cathedral.

73 Abū Ḥamīd al-Ghazālī, 'The Beginning of Guidance', trans. W. Montgomery Watt in *The Faith and Practice of Al-Ghazālī*, op. cit., p. 127.

73 Egyptian Christian papyrus, *Patrologia Latina*, 18:442, in *Early Christian Prayers*, op. cit., p. 94.

74 Aḥmad ibn Idrīs, *Prayers*.

74 Henry Suso, 'The Exemplar', in *Life and Writings of the Blessed Henry Suso*, ed. Nicholas Heller, trans. M. A. Edward (Dubuque, Iowa, U.S.A., The Priory Press, 1962) Vol. 1, p. 25.

74 Lancelot Andrewes, *Preces Privatae*, in *Lancelot Andrewes and his Private Devotions*, op. cit., pp. 79–80.

75 Abū Ḥamīd al-Ghazālī, *Prayer of the Prophet Muḥammad*, in *Majallat al-Azhar*, Ramaḍān, 1387 A.H. (A.D. 1967), Vol. 39, No. 7.

76 Christopher Smart, 'On the Eternity of the Supreme Being', in *Collected Poems*, ed. N. Callan (London, Routledge and Kegan Paul, 1949) Vol. 1, pp. 227–30.

77 Henry Suso, 'The Exemplar', in *Life and Writings of the Blessed Henry Suso*, op. cit., Vol. 1, p. 25.

78 Henry Suso, ibid.

page

78 Thomas Traherne, *Thanksgiving for the Body* in *Centuries, Poems, and Thanksgivings*, op. cit., Vol ii, pp. 218, 220, 221 (lines 143–52, 158–60, 242, 254–65).

79 ʿAbd al-Qādir al-Jīlānī, 'Wells of Prayer', in *Muslim Devotions*, op. cit., p. 254.

79 Ibn Ḥazm, *The Ring of the Dove*, trans. A. J. Arberry (London, Luzac and Co., 1953) p. 177.

80 John S. Hoyland, *The Fourfold Sacrament* (Cambridge, Heffer, second edition, 1924) p. 67.

80 George Campbell, 'Litany', from *Caribbean Voices* Vol. 1: *Dreams and Visions*, ed. John Figueroa (London, Evans Brothers, 1967) p. 27.

81 ʿAbd al-ʿAzīz al-Dīrīnī, 'Purity of Heart', trans. C. E. Padwick in *Muslim Devotions*, op. cit., p. 219.

81 P. B. Shelley, *The Witch of Atlas*, stanzas LXI–LXII, in *The Complete Poetical Works of Percy Bysshe Shelley*, ed. Thomas Hutchinson (London, Oxford University Press, 1905) p. 379.

81 *The Book of Common Prayer*, The Third Collect at Evening Prayer.

82 Milton, *Paradise Lost*, Bk. iii, lines 60–3.

82 P. Gerhardt, *Hymn at Nightfall* trans. 'Y.H.' (Robert Bridges in *Yattendon Hymnal*; v. 3 omitted by permission).

83 *Ramaḍān Prayers*, in *Mukhtaṣar Adʿiyat Ramaḍān* (Sidon, Lebanon, 1930).

83 *Patrologia Orientalis*, 24:670.

84 Invocations from *Ḥirz al-Jawsh*.

84 Abū-l-ʿAlā al-Maʿarī, *Poems*, trans. H. Baerlein (London, John Murray, 1914) No. xiii, pp. 85-6.

84 Thomas Traherne, *Centuries, Poems, and Thanksgivings*, op. cit., Vol. i, pp. 102, 104 (Second Century, 90, 92).

85 Aʿbd al-Laṭīf al-Baghdādī, *Kitāb al-Ifādah wa-l-Iʿtibār* (Paris, 1810) pp. 152, 154.

PENITENCE

page

96 Tradition noted by Ibn Ḥazm, *The Ring of the Dove*, op. cit., p. 281.

96 Stephen Crane, 'War is Kind', in *The Work of Stephen Crane*, ed. W. Follet (New York, Russell and Russell Inc., 1895) Vol. 6, p. 121, No. 12.

97 Hugh Latimer, *Sermons* ed. John Watkins (1824) Vol. 1, p. 123.

97 Arthur Hugh Clough, 'The Latest Decalogue', in *Poetical Works*, ed. F. T. Palgrave (London, Routledge and Sons, 1906) p. 44.

98 Ezra Pound, First Pisan Canto, *The Pisan Cantos* (London, Faber and Faber, 1949) p. 7, lines 1–2.

98 Mufakrul-Islām, *Bengali Poems*.

99 Matthew 25:42–5.

99 Jalāl al-Dīn Rūmī, *Tales from the Mathnawī*, trans. A. J. Arberry (London, Allen and Unwin, 1961) p. 42.

100 Aḥmad ibn Idris, *Prayers*, *Aḥzāb wa Awrād*.

100 Aḥmad Bashaikh ibn Ḥusain, 'Shairit waa baruwa', trans. Lyndon Harries, in *Swahili Poetry* (London, Oxford University Press, 1964), pp. 259–61 (stanzas 6–8).

101 John S. Hoyland, *The Fourfold Sacrament*, op. cit., p. 67.

101 *Pilgrimage Prayers*, op. cit.

101 Abū Hamīd al-Ghazālī, *The Reviving of Religion*, op. cit., 1.9, pp. 287–8.

103 Shenute, *Coptic Prayers of Dair al-Abyad*, Egypt, in *Early Christian Prayers*, op. cit., pp. 191–2.

103 Amīr Hamzah, *In Darkness*, trans. A. H. Johns, in *Malayan and Indonesian Studies*, ed. John Bastin and R. Roolvink (Oxford, Clarendon Press, 1964) p. 319.

103 Invocations from *Ḥirz al-Jawsh*.

104 Aḥmad al-Tījānī, *Prayers*.

105 Albert Camus in *The Fall*, trans. Justin O'Brien (London, Heinemann, 1957), pp. 101, 103.

105 John Donne, 'Good Friday, Riding Westward' in *Poetical Works*, ed. H. J. C. Grierson (Oxford, Clarendon Press, 1912) Vol. 1, p. 337, lines 39–42.

PETITION

page

108 Invocations from *Ḥirz al-Jawsh*.

109 'Utendi wa Mwana Kupona', trans. Lyndon Harries, in *Swahili Poetry*, op. cit., pp. 73, 75, 85.

109 Abū Ḥamīd al-Ghazālī, *The Reviving of Religion*, op. cit.,

110 Tradition of the Prophet, noted by Muslim and by Ibn Khaldūn. See *Al-Muqaddimah*, ed. F. Rosenthal (London, Routledge & Kegan Paul, 1958) Vol. i, Ch. 3, Section 6.

111 Walt Whitman, 'I Sit and Look Out', in *Leaves of Grass* (London, Siegle Hill and Co., 1907) pp. 179–80.

112 Thomas Cranmer, The English Litany: *Book of Common Prayer*.

113 Shamsur Raḥmān, *Poems of East Bengal*, trans. Yusuf Jamal Begum, in *Presenting Pakistani Poetry*, op. cit., p. 88.

113 Ibn ʿAbdus, 'Sword and Lance', in *Moorish Poetry*, trans. A. J. Arberry, op. cit., p. 63.

113 Prayer at the close of *Ṣalāt*.

113 Claude McKay, 'The Pagan Isms', in *Caribbean Voices*, Vol. 1: *Dreams and Visions*, op. cit., p. 100.

114 ʿIyād Ibn Mūsā, 'Corn in the Wind', in *Moorish Poetry*, trans. A. J. Arberry, op. cit., p. 124.

114 Clement of Rome, *Epistle to the Corinthians*, LX–LXI, in *Opera Patrum Apostolicorum*, ed. F. X. Funk (Tubingen, 1887), Vol. i, p. 134.

115 Colossians 3:15.

115 Anonymous, Somaliland, 'Camel Watering Chant', trans. B. W. Andrzejewski and I. M. Lewis, in *Somali Poetry: An Introduction* (Oxford, Clarendon Press, 1964), p. 140.

115 Dag Hammarskjöld, *Markings*, op. cit., p. 123.

116 Zuhair, poet of the Jāhiliyyah, *Muʿallaqah*, in C. J. Lyall: *Translations of Ancient Arabic Poetry* (second edition 1930), p. 113.

page

116 Poem of the Jāhiliyyah, *The Banū Zimman*, in C. J. Lyall, op. cit., p. 5.

116 Francis of Assisi.

116 Ibn al-Ḥajj, in *Moorish Poetry*, trans. A. J. Arberry, op. cit., p. 131.

117 2 Corinthians 6:12–13.

117 W. B. Yeats, *Collected Poems* (London, Macmillan and Co., 1950) p. 288.

118 Jalāl al-Dīn Rūmī, *Mathnawī*, trans. R. A. Nicholson (London, 1925), Vol. 1, p. 180.

119 Wisdom of Solomon (Apocrypha) 2:12–22.

120 Eugene Ionesco, *Notes and Counter Notes*, trans. D. Watson (London, Calder, 1964) p. 160.

122 Josh Malihabādī, 'Our Society', trans. M. A. Seljuk, in *Presenting Pakistani Poetry*, ed. G. Allama, op. cit., p. 15.

122 Alexander Blok, in *Modern Russian Poetry*, trans. V. Markov and M. Sparks (London, MacGibbon and Kee Ltd., 1966) p. 179.

123 Fyodor I. Tyutchev, in *Poems from the Russian*, trans. F. Cornford and E. P. Salaman (London, Faber and Faber, 1943) p. 46.

124 Balai, of Aleppo, Syriac Hymn for a church hallowing, in *Early Christian Prayers*, ed. Adalbert Hamman, op. cit., p. 187.

124 Abū Ḥamīd al-Ghazālī, *Al-Munqidh min al-Ḍalāl*, final prayer, (Cairo edition, 1309 A.H.).

125 Muḥammad Iqbāl, *Jāvīd Nāmā*, trans. A. J. Arberry (London, Allen and Unwin, 1966) lines 1061, 1063, 1064, 1066.

125 *Prayers of the Naqshabandī Order*.

126 Clement of Rome, *Epistle to the Corinthians*, LIX–LX, in *Opera Patrum Apostolicorum*, op. cit., Vol. 1, p. 134.

127 *Te Deum Laudamus* (conclusion), Morning Prayer, *Book of Common Prayer*.

page

127 Aḥmad al-Tijānī, *Prayers*.

128 Abū-l-ʿAlā al-Maʿarī, *Quatrains* XIV, XXIV, XXV, from *The Diwan of Abū-l-ʿAlā*, trans. Henry Baerlein, (London, John Murray, 1913).

128 ʿAbdul-Halīm Josh, 'Let us forward go' trans. from Sindhi by G. Allama, in *Presenting Pakistani Poetry*, op. cit., p. 124.

128 John Bunyan, *The Pilgrim Song* (adapted).

129 Matthew 5:44–5.

129 Sirāj of Andalusia, in *Moorish Poetry*, trans. A. J. Arberry, op. cit., p. 65.

129 Ibn Tufayl, concluding prayer in *Alive, Son of Alert*, ed. A. Amin (Cairo, 1952) p. 131.

129 Albert Camus, *The Plague*, trans. Stuart Gilbert (London, Penguin Books, 1960) p. 186.

130 Bertolt Brecht, 'Die Ausnahme und die Regel', in *Stücke*, Vol. 5, ed. E. Burri and E. Hauptmann (Berlin, 1957), p. 187.

131 Stephen Crane, 'War is Kind', in *The Work of Stephen Crane*, op. cit., Vol. 6, p. 131, No. xxii.

132 Aleksei K. Gastev, *Modern Russian Poetry*, trans. V. Markov and M. Sparks, op. cit., p. 699.

133 John Donne, 'Third Satire', in *Poetical Works*, ed. H. J. C. Grierson (Oxford, Clarendon Press, 1912) Vol. 1, p. 158, lines 100–2.

134 Ezra Pound, Canto XLV: *With Usura, The Cantos of Ezra Pound* (London, Faber and Faber, 1964) pp. 239–40.

135 Thomas Traherne, *Centuries, Poems, and Thanksgivings*, op. cit., VI of *Christian Ethics*, pp. 187–8, lines 1, 10–11, 14–18, 19–21, 23–30.

136 Ezra Pound, 'Commission', in *Personae: Collected Shorter Poems* (London, Faber and Faber, 1952) pp. 97–8.

137 Richard Crashaw, 'To the Countess of Denbigh', in *Poems*, ed. A. R. Waller (Cambridge University Press, 1904) pp. 190–2.

page

138 Lancelot Andrewes, *Preces Privatae*, in *Lancelot Andrewes and his Private Devotions*, op. cit., pp. 99–103.

138 Invocations from *Ḥirz al-Jawsh*.

139 Ibn Ḥazm, *The Ring of the Dove*, op. cit., p. 181.

140 Matthew 6:33 (AV/KJV).

140 Kāmil Ḥussein, *City of Wrong*, trans. Kenneth Cragg (Amsterdam, Djambatan, 1959) p. 132.

141 Dennis Osadebay, from *West African Verse*, ed. D. I. Nwoga (London, Longmans, Green and Co., 1967) p. 15.

142 Shams al-Dīn Ḥāfīẓ, 'Wild Deer', trans. A. J. Arberry in *Fifty Poems of Hafiz* (London, Cambridge University Press, 1947) p. 131.

142 Abū Ḥamīd al-Ghazālī, *The Reviving of Religion*, op. cit., p. 34.

143 Léopold Sédar Senghor, 'Night in Senegal', in *Selected Poems* trans. John Reed and Clive Wake (London, Oxford University Press, 1964) p. 5.

143 Léopold Sédar Senghor, 'Prayer for Peace', in *Selected Poems*, op. cit., p. 51.

144 Jalāl al-Dīn Rūmī, *Mathnawi*, trans. R. A. Nicholson, *op. cit.* Vol. 1, lines 3069–73.

144 Walt Whitman, 'To Think of Time', in *Leaves of Grass*, op. cit., p. 386.

145 Ezra Pound, 'Dieu Qui l'a Faicte', in *Personae: Collected Shorter Poems*, op. cit., p. 84.

145 Abū-l-ʿAlā al-Maʿarī, *Letters of Abū-l-ʿAlā al-Maʿari*, trans. D. S. Margoliouth (Oxford, Clarendon Press, 1898) No. 31, p. 133.

146 Abū-l-ʿAlā al-Maʿarī, ibid., Nos. 30, 35, 38 (2), and 41; pp. 132–3, 137, 140–1, and 144.

147 George Campbell, 'Jamaica Constitution Day Poem', in *Caribbean Voices* Vol. I: *Dreams and Visions*, op. cit., p. 67.

148 Muhammad Iqbāl, *Jāvīd Nāmā*, op. cit., lines 1477–8.

148 George Campbell, 'Holy', in *Caribbean Voices* Vol. I: *Dreams and Visions*, op. cit., p. 94.

page

148 1 Corinthians 3:16–17.

149 Michel Quoist, 'The Pornographic Magazine' in *Prayers of Life* (Dublin, Gill and Macmillan Ltd., 1965) p. 25.

150 Hilāl Nājī, *The Worshipper of the Flesh*.

150 Jalāl al-Dīn Rūmī, *Discourses*, trans. A. J. Arberry, op. cit., p. 28.

151 Michel Quoist, 'Eyes' in *Prayers of Life*, op. cit., pp. 35–7.

151 Shāh ʿAbdul Laṭīf, 'Obstinate Eyes', trans. G. Allama, in *Presenting Pakistani Poetry*, op. cit., p. 104.

152 Alexander Pushkin, 'The Coach of Life', in *Poems from the Russian* trans. F. Cornford and E. P. Salaman (London, Faber and Faber, 1943) p. 16.

153 Ezra Pound, 'The Return' in *Personae: Collected Shorter Poems*, op. cit., p. 85.

153 Ibn Ḥazm, *The Ring of the Dove*, trans. A. J. Arberry, op. cit., p. 174.

153 Karl Rahner, *Prayers for Meditation*, op. cit., p. 71.

154 *Corpus Inscriptionum Latinarum*, Vol. ii: 4964.

154 *Pilgrimage Prayers*, *Manāsik al-Ḥajj wa Adʿiyat-al-Tawāf*, op. cit.

154 Egyptian Commendation (5th century), trans. by the Editor from *Dictionnaire d'Archaeologie Chrétienne et de Liturgie* (ed. Cabrol et Leclercq) Vol. 14: 1769.

154 *Monumenta Ecclesiae Liturgica*, trans. by the Editor (ed. Cabrol et Leclercq) No. CXVIII.

155 Abū Ḥamīd al-Ghazālī, 'Morning Prayer of Abraham', in *The Reviving of Religion, Iḥyā ʿUlūm al-Dīn*, op. cit., I. 9, p. 285.

155 Dag Hammarskjöld, *Markings*, op. cit., p. 93.

155 Ancient Irish Prayer.

156 Søren Kierkegaard, *Journals*, op. cit., pp. 172–3.

156 Fakhr al-Dīn al-Rāzī, 'The Clear and the Shining', in *Muslim Devotions*, op. cit., pp. 123–4.

Index of Authors and Sources

Index of Themes of Prayer

Index of Quranic Passages

(The Surahs are cited by titles as in the text. The serial numbers follow in brackets.)

Index of Biblical Passages